JEWGIRL

Also by Charlene Fix

Taking a Walk in My Animal Hat
Frankenstein's Flowers
Harpo Marx as Trickster
Charlene Fix's Greatest Hits: 1998-2011
Flowering Bruno: a Dography
Mischief

JEWGIRL

Stubborn and stiff-necked man! the Rabbi cried.
* The pain you give me, said I.*
Instead of bowing down, said he,
You go on in your obstinacy.
* We Jews are that way, I replied.*

Howard Nemerov, *Debate with the Rabbi*

CHARLENE FIX
Poems

Broadstone

Library of Congress Control No. 2023944758

ISBN 978-1-956782-50-9

Text & Cover Design by Larry W. Moore

Cover artwork:
Golden Afternoon by Nora Kobrinsky,
used by permission

Author photography by Sonya Fix

Broadstone Books
An Imprint of
Broadstone Media LLC
418 Ann Street
Frankfort, KY 40601-1929
BroadstoneBooks.com

for Margie, Sandy, and Irene, with love

CONTENTS

I. *Nexus*

II. *Slow Learning*

V. *Heart and Soul*

I.

Nexus

ONIONS

My father used to call my sister and me *tsibeles*,
which is Yiddish for *onions*. The man was a poet,
and this may have been his only poem.
We don't know what he meant, but it's too late
to ask him. With our mother he would bathe us,
saying, at times, *stand up so I can wash your business*,
which amounts to another poem, now that I
think about it, one whose implications may
have carried him to onions, small ones, pungent,
and with secrets deep within, such as we were.

~

Today a friend declares he is an onion
whose layers would peel down to nothing.
That he thinks this is sad, but it makes me
remember I'm an onion too; it steers me
to the memory of my father's one-word poem,
tsibeles, and other tentacled thoughts. Even
while we talk, my mind is distracted by
the green slip of a sprout one finds deep
inside an onion. So it doesn't peel down
to nothing after all, but to that slight stem,
that little life inside the layers, and the lovely
way the layers overlap, arms enfolding one
another like soft shields over not-nothing,
like wings, and the wings of wings,
and the wings of wings of wings.

AFRICA PARTY

I eye the fish on the table.
It looks so dry, so dark, so
shriveled that I'm not sure
it is a fish. I only suspect.
But when my neighbor, young
devoted third-grade teacher,
rips its hide with his fingers,
yanking off flesh to eat on
a cracker, I do too. Ice broken,
so to speak, others eat it now—
ripe old smoky fish: symbol
and sign. For this is a Christian
party to collect money for Africa
where every day two thousand
children die of malaria, as if
each day the sun comes up,
the towers fall, and down go
two more thousand lives. My
husband cannot bring himself
here, being still in recovery
from grade-school photographs
of "pagan babies," and little
boxes for coins to save "the
pagan babies' souls." But I,
who spent the green years running
with my own and others' sacrosanct
un-christened souls, am happy
someone is counting and go.

APRIL FOOLS

Today is called April Fools' Day
but I needn't know why. I have
my own theory. The sun is shining on mud.
Long winter, puffy coat dragging,
is backing away. The mud is opening.
Leaves are checking arrival schedules,
branches full of suspense, while fools
are stepping forward into spring
in a particularly violent time, so much work
to be done in the world. And it's the sweet fools—
little girls climbing into school buses,
doctors and nurses heading straight for rubble and plagues,
anonymous artists writing grafitti on barrier walls,
those who lean relatively small shoulders
against mired wheels—who will do it.
I have lost faith in spiffy high achievers
who can't draw a straight line from the heart.
The greedy and the partisan are not fools. Fools
forget calculators, they smile at the small, they refuse
to parse love. Fools are like swallows just before dusk
soaring north, then south, east, then west,
making parabolas in the sky, looping over traffic,
over peeling bricks and potholed roads with no agenda.
They are simply playing—we have to call this playing.
Or we can call it the alacrity, the daring sweep, of fools.

Unobservant Jew

My own personal Rabbi, Walt Whitman, sifted
the grist of this peopled continent and thus
made palpable *the oversoul*. But here I am,
such an unobservant Jew that I didn't even notice
today was Yom Kippur, so I ate a sandwich
on the way to work, having spread peanut butter
on some silly slices of white wholewheat I bought
accidentally, being an unobservant shopper too,
rolling down the bread aisle at Kroger singing songs
in my head. Also on this Yom Kippur I had an esthetic
lunch at the museum, then went home to let the dog out
in the yard where I picked my very own raspberries,
placing each one between nobody's lips but mine.
Later I ate a dinner consisting of salmon patties,
a salad, and a baked potato, before sundown of course,
and my husband ate of this too, though he is both
observant and not a Jew. After all this eating,
I suddenly remembered it was a fast day, holy
like each day is holy, only more so.

Let me try to say all this another way. If I
walked to your house in the rain, then entered
your study to learn from you, and you asked me
on which side of my boots I had placed my umbrella,
I wouldn't be able to tell you, so you'd be justified
in dismissing me. But I do know that every day
somewhere people are going without food,
which makes every day *Yom Kippur*, holy
only more so, full of fasting and atonement
in this *overly-soulful* world.

COUNTRY AND COUNTRY

in memory of Eric

We were taking lots of rides beyond the city then,
past grounded clouds gauzing a heaven of hazy colts,

past mares and meditative cows, and even an occasional
deer grazing wild among them. But you grew confused

when we called this *country*, for you had learned in school
that many *countries* make the world. Yours was America.

How we labored to explain the fullness of the word,
but you folded your six-years' length of arms across your heart,

dismissing us with a skeptical drift of cobalt blue eyes.
You live now way beyond the clouds, in another country

where, at last, we'll all set down our valises full of abstractions
and, like immigrants, take a good look around.

Some will expect winding streets, cafes, and dogs
napping two by two in squares. May they find them.

Others will seek fields of flax and oats, and animals
no hand will ever mar *davening* in fields near open roads,

where deep magenta ironweed shares slopes with orange lilies.

The Burial of Bruno Schulz

Under a streetlamp impersonating the moon
but without the moon's broad face of pity, bland and blind,

I slide one arm around the shoulder of my friend,
the other under knees that give and bend

to lift him from the gutter's iridescent stream,
and leave the other dead like fish afloat in blood and gasoline.

His bones drum on the taut skin of my heart.
His dreams eke out, flowers of black smoke that bloom and disappear.
I lurch like geriatric gears.

A horn blares. Must be fast. The armed and uniformed and bored
are trying to blunt the horror of these executions, executing more.

Here's the shovel, leaning on a tree.
We bury the murdered in collusion, secretly.
He hid his manuscripts like footprints in the moss and leaves.

I dig. He leans in catatonic meditation on his state, an empty sack.
Once full, he dived; we followed him; he blew us back.

The horse of childhood offers greetings, four feet in the air,
fleeing to where the planets sag and antic stars are spare.

KAFKA'S SISTER

The far right is rising again in Austria / as the shadow of Ottla, Kafka's sister /
floats over Terezin and then Auschwitz / where she was gassed / with a
thousand children. Mary Crow

One can only imagine her
     in Terezin, plucking
          lice from her shirt,

the lifestyle mirrored
     above the hill of her nose
          in her eye lakes.

Her brother, dead,
     could not be blamed
          for the wild dishabille.

Blame thick roots, rather,
     of Czechoslovak soil
          that roiled around their seed

while that seed bred,
     blame forests, clay,
          a moist God

who was both
     celebrated and denied.
          Her people knew

about weeds in the brain,
     those flowering non-flowers
          ruggedly designed,

and how tightening
     tightens but loosening
          loosens the noose.

She used to be amused
     by what her brother thought
          on strange sheets,

but here she learned
 how like their God, who can't
  be looked upon

if one would live, was truth.
 Yet he spent himself
  dragging it into light.

SAGA OF MICE

after Art Spiegelman's *Maus*

I imagine the mice in my daughter's apartment
walking around with huge bellies and tiny towels
draped over their shoulders, for they have found
the good life in Flatbush, Brooklyn.

In a matter of days they emptied
an unopened bag of cat food under the sink,
chewed through two layers of plastic
and consumed a quantity unimaginable for mice.
They must be thirsty now, I think.

All their names are *Moishele*, for they
wandered deserts of walls and pipes
before they found oasis under this sink.
Then they jumped into the moment of opulence
with little mouse feet, *fressing* and *shmoozing*.

The day before, one of their own had been taken in thrall
by Indira: charming, indifferent cat,
batted into a stupor, then left to die among
stuffed mice, twine balls, and other toys
while the others wept and shrilled.

My daughter says she heard them screaming
while the episode endured. So here it is again:
ambition's motor: fear. I picture them in *tallit*,
davening, feasting as only the bereft can feast,
pleasure both intensified and hollowed out by grief.

Adiós, Don Quixote

I often slept oblivious of your sandwiched escapades,
'til worries I could not assimilate startled me awake.
Then you held your horses for me, you in pie pan armor,

my bedside lamp transformed to 16th century Spanish sun.
For years we rode the rocky, green, and wooded miles,
you on Rocinante, Sancho on Dapple, I upon a mattress

that could buck with fears. I hid with you from agitated hours
because no rain fell on your day-for-night, your life-correcting plain,
O effervescently abiding old school gentleman

who got back on your horse after blows and falls!
Sojourning in the land my forbears loved but had to leave,
I basked in those ancestral rays, partaking of your olives, bread, and cheese,

stopping with you at inns. Your horses were your friends,
as they became each other's. As for us, *Señor*, page eight hundred thirty
just expelled me too, from a place that soothes and heals for being far removed.

Perhaps I could wade in that Spanish river twice, by which I mean
the funny curving path you ride. *Pero no puedo.* I'm due in other worlds
before the light grows dim, feet first with painted toenails.

You spent the tender of your mad brave self without depletion
until the inevitable guy who knew you when put the kibosh on self-invention.
Felicitaciones, Don Quixote, for resisting so long!

Ivanhoe

My daughter left me propped on pillows
and tiptoed out while I kept reading,
hooked by paper intimates who would
walk with me a while in the world.

A Jewish father had a daughter who had
eyes like crater lakes. She had a knight
regarding her who had an affianced.
They coped with inquisitions, contests,
fire and forbearance, greed and grace.

I was also hooked by the artifact itself,
for as I turned each page, it forsook the others,
fell to the floor among the starched leaves
from that Romantic tree, now strangers.

Or you could say the book parted like waters,
offered up the redolence of currents
from another world, let me lave in them,
then evaporated like history's rain, leaving
nothing between the covers, for *Ivanhoe*
gave itself to me like no book had before.

AFTER "AFTER APPLE-PICKING"

I wondered if the ice skimmed from the trough
through which the poet gazed upon his world
might be the lens of death that warps perception.
I was more certain that the apples rolling in,
some with imperfections on their skins,
were metaphors for poems, the poem itself
a sensuous grand allegory for the poet's work—
I knew this, do not ask me how, nineteen,
a toddler in the universe-city, yet
my Professor said, "there's insufficient
evidence to justify this reading."

Back then I thought that he and I were kin,
our noses shaped the same, his surname
like my grandfather's before he swapped it
on Ellis Island for a name betokening
a priestly caste of Jews. My fondness for
my Prof, his intellect, remains. I send him essays,
never poems. I mention this because
a recent article by someone else in *APR*
proposed my "After Apple Picking" theme.
But more, because tonight I heard a high
school girl recite—nay, vivify—Frost's poem.

When I return to Denney Hall at OSU,
dark unlovely though it is, where I became
myself by way of Transcendentalism,
I play a game with my own head. If I enter
through the east door, ride that elevator up,
the English Department office sprawls on the left.
But if I enter through the west door, ride up there,
it's on the right. In this way I make
the mighty fourth floor flip, proving nothing
doesn't change with one's emergent point of view.

An undergrad, I gazed with awe at the portals
to Parnassus, those faculty mailboxes
beside a barrier only the anointed could cross.
A graduate T.A., I had a magic mailbox too,
and was allowed to lift the drawbridge
by its hinge. In that way I learned there wasn't
much ado beyond the counter.

GARDENIAS

for Billy Holiday, as all gardenias must forever be

When a flower visits you three times in three days,
a flower you have met before but barely remember,
you have to consider the synchronicity,
that this might be the Universe *yoo-hooing* to you
in a form involuted and sexy and coded and perfumy,
though there's always the possibility you can touch
and smell and pore over such a thing for weeks and not get it:
this is how people go mad, this may be the Universe toying with you.

One day I'm ironing, a housewifely thing to do, though most
of the clothes in the basket are mine, while watching an old sitcom
with prejudices manifested by the utter absence of the richly hued;
they're simply not there, nowhere, like Jews suddenly suitcased
and on their way to vacations in hell, a silence reminiscent also
of the meowing of our old cat Ribby who would beg to come in
through the beveled glass, her mouth open in a plaint we couldn't hear.

So I'm ironing, and it seems Wally wants to buy his mercenary date
a gardenia but his dad says *no*, though the interesting thing is
the dad changes his mind, and this is hopeful: at first, he's adamant,
self-righteous, yet he changes his mind when the dressed-up-at-home
wife shows him a squooshed gardenia in a thick book from a date long ago,
ho hum, a real splurge, and he is about to call the fellow who bought it
a *fool* when he realizes he was him.

Then the next day I'm minding my own business, flipping
magazine pages when suddenly photos of fancy white gardenias
pounce upon me in a variety of shapes, for they have adapted
where they grew, and I'd say more but I threw out the magazine,
even though normally I keep such things around forever, but who
knew I was going to try to comprehend what the Universe
was telling me via gardenias, go figure.

And if you do, call me so I can lend this coherence,
having tossed the magazine one day before the third encounter,
when I was watching *A Day at the Races* for the umpteenth time

because those guys were onto something, and in one scene
Groucho has a big blonde up in his room at the sanitarium
where he is posing as a people doctor but is really
a veterinarian so as to placate and woo the hypochondriac
rich lady who can't tell the difference between physical
and mental suffering, as most of us can't. So Groucho
keeps saying *thank you* in a funny way to the blonde broad—
now there's a word! Right out of the thirties, such a ring,
and by the way, did you ever notice how many synonyms
there are for women while hardly any for men? But never mind,
that's a digression, let's drop it, even though these are all digressions,
which, I hope, are getting us closer to solving the mystery of gardenias,
why they called to me three days running, a flower I never
paid much mind and probably won't again.
So there's Groucho offering the blonde dame a gardenia,
but, whoops, it's not a gardenia but some cheap clownish peony,
though what does he care? He knows this is just a fling, but
thank goodness for the sanitarium and Margaret Dumont
that his brothers aren't buying it and wallpaper over the blonde.

Now you might think that's the end of it. I have told you
three loping sagas of gardenias. But I just remembered
a fourth and perhaps the sweetest of all: *Jungle Gardenia*,
my favorite perfume when I was a teenager and knew
simply nothing, and had a bottle of *Shalimar*, much classier,
more expensive, but one day my buddy Barb knocked me out
with the scent she had on, and I ran right to the drug store
to buy some—it was heady and exotic and musky and cheap,
and in truth I preferred it. So some days I'd be classy
and wear *Shalimar*, but other days I'd be slutty in my dreams
and wear *Jungle Gardenia*, with my stockings, pumps,
and straight skirt, all girdled in, sweatered but without
the requisite big breasts, though inside I was all pink and glowing,
and gardenia-scented I would lean breathless on a locker
in a noisy, slushy (it snowed a lot in Cleveland) hall.

BURNING BUSH

It was an ordinary day.
My husband left at 7:00 for his job,
my son at 7:10 for school.
I ate some toast, tidied up,
then walked the dog at 8:00.
He stopped at every bush to smell the news.
I didn't mind our pace. The morning sun,
the creeping of that distant radiance,
was worth a pause, for in the winter
it is elsewhere more than it is here.

Thinned by mist, light painted
and the shapes of things emerged:
my sleeves, a neighbor's bits of bread for birds,
a hydrant and a paper cup. I could say
light ignited into fire the very bush
before which Bruno raised his leg.
I could say *orange light on ruddy wood*
swaying in wind struck senses like a flame.
And I could thus imply God spoke.

No flame. Just barren trees and bushes' bones,
and this one lilac bush with embryonic
buds that formed before the winter fell,
before the winter fell way back in June,
when purple clusters streamed with scent
and we breathed deeply as we passed.

Sonnet for Bears

December bells, bidding us to buy
stuffed bears, are tolling for the Jersey bears
run like deer though lumbering under
the sky. Some genius' solution to
suburban conflict: bears must die. They hunch
their backs in forests, teach the *Shoah* to
their young, eating grains unleavened, drinking
grapes before they're wine. *Kaddish* winds
are *davening* the pines while picketers
are hoisting photographs of dignitary
bears, ears round as *yarmulkes*, on signs.
Just when the days seem normal, people start
to murder once again, this time what
should please them most: morphs of dogs and men.

Sasha and the Bees

They're plump this time of year,
and it is sweet—so much depends
upon the bumblebees—to see
them supping at the daffodils.
And Sasha's plump, or plumper
than she used to be. Once,
while zooming in the yard,
she tried to eat a bee. It stung;
she cried; she swelled, yet now I see
her poking with her paw a hobbled bee
and nosing it, then trying to snap one
from the air, a crunch that may be
worth the risk, or else she can't sustain
a grudge, like Gimpel, and like me.

NEXUS

summer, 2014

From nature's slow vigor a wasp withdraws
to a patch of sunlight on the wide arm

of the Adirondack chair. I'm not sure why
it has landed so near my own darkening limb

that is minding its own business, juicy and biteable.
A telephone and glass of water sit on the other side,

and a book lies open in my lap: everything
Middle Eastern this summer: novels, poems

from various persuasions there, the human nuance
buried in the news. Here it is quiet:

the raging sun soundless, clouds silently
striating the enigmatic blue,

the novel not speaking unless spoken to,
the water reflecting circling dreams.

The wasp's exhaustion has made of us friends.
Its segmented body is clinging to the wood,

and its antennae are waving, swayed, perhaps,
by wind. Its back faces me

as if it is driving our chair into eternity,
head low to gaze on the mysteries multiplying

in the shade of the yew. I'm here for no
other reason than I'm here, while the wasp,

its wings dripping the bliss of mortality,
has chosen to abide by me so will not die alone.

MARIA

In your long and lonely days as a Greek immigrant
on American shores, your mother's words
came back to you, flowing into the ear of your own silence.
The ocean breeze carried the present away.

Your mother's dying words, her ashen face
as she held you, caressed you, her mouth speaking
to her tiny Maria, fearing that Maria's life would be a broken shell.

Did your mother have eyes like yours, warm and brown,
full of knowledge gleaned in boats, wharves, villages,
through childbirth, welfare, madness,
distinct from the drama, the thought, the art
that before you were Greek to me?

You were Greek, Maria. Your mother starved
during the war so her children might eat, so Maria
could become a woman and venture to America,
to weep over a husband with a bum arm who couldn't work,
and sew thick coats in a factory until she slowly stopped eating
and only prayed, not leaving the bed for months,
praying continuously, until God said, "Get up, Maria."

Your mother died while Hitler was in Greece.
You saw him when you were small and her body
was rejecting the few crusts she claimed, so when
I told you I was a Jew, your Mediterranean eyes
warmed the cold ashes in me.

In Greece, your husband, in passion, locked you in the house
and carried the key with him. But by America, his bum arm,
and your talent for surviving, he was tamed.

Your sons are runners by the sea. They do not remember
the Easter lamb in your Greek village, nor the lemons
big as oranges. Your husband fishes on this side

of the ocean now. You dig small crabs for bait on the beach.
The warm salt breezes ruffle your hair. Sunlight
warms your back and tans your face and arms,
while your children grow tall and strong in an American slum.

RHONDA IS STARING AT ME

after The Blue Mountain *by Meir Shalev*

I'm on the high new bed
I need a Sherpa to ascend,
or if the Sherpa's on a break,
a grappling hook. The nightstand
hovers far below. I slide
to the center, suspended on
layers of cotton, wool, foam,
afloat in the virtual world
of a Palestinian/Israeli novel
wherein the eyes of cows brim
with tears when they behold
the butcher, and a mule
knocks on the door of his
human nemesis, seeking revenge.
Now Rhonda is crossing the floor
and leaping to the bench, her
pointed ears, the closely gathered
features of her feline face a moon
rising over the foot of the bed.
Up she springs to tread on me
regardless of geography or history,
not content to sprawl at my side
but settling on my heart, then
inching forward until her paws
stretch to my neck, her eyes
staring into mine.

WRITERS ARE THE HEROES OF THE WORLD

because manifold truth runs through narrative,
even while narratives spar. Winners frame the stories,

but losers whisper theirs into rivers, sending them
down currents in script of bubbles and foam.

Like the mad with their chips and directives,
we stick to our versions even when drenched

by tsunamis of disbelief or evidence to the contrary.
Boys who assault girls barely in their teens

think sexual terrorism a joke on the status
of women, the prerogatives of men.

Those who wave confederate flags compel faces
to morph into stone, a preemptive move against

white fog and what it brings. It even happens
that the yellow stars my people were forced to wear

can be dyed black and repurposed for blinders.
Yet writers, sweating and brave, climb down

from their own laps to dive into tumultuous waters,
parsing oxygen from hydrogen in order to breathe,

making bioluminescent friends in order to see.
Turning and turning in the weightlessness that is the sea,

they wash up panting on shores far and near, seaweed, shells, bones
of various schools transcribed in their fins, fingers, fists.

II.

Slow Learning

DEPUTIZED

At high noon, Will Kane
threw down in the dust his yellow star,
mounted buckboard, rode away.

But when Nazis deputized Jews,
pinning on them yellow stars,
they couldn't refuse.

Under piss-yellow cloth,
under shirts, coats, skin,
they were forced to assert
imperatives of kin.

So the pins that joined the stars to them
keep penetrating: slim, terrible, sharp,
all the way to the rising, deflating
bread of the heart.

You Carried Her in Your Arms

You carried her in your arms back to our house,
having found her, frail and old, collapsed on the sidewalk.
She wasn't dead, but she was hard to revive.

I lay down on the carpet next to her as if she were a cat.
When she stirred, I offered her orange juice
instead of water. She took a few sips, sat, stood up,

pronounced herself well, then told us a lie: that she
had merely been out walking, circling the block
with every intention of ending up at the house of a friend.

You carried her in your arms although you didn't know
who or what she was, as I have carried in my heart's arms
childhood chums with parents who had numbers

needled on their skin. The old woman wasn't dressed
for a commemoration, but that was where she was
expected to be, an honoree representing a generation

of genocide survivors. I knew this because I went
out on the street to ask passers-by. It was falling
to me to get her there, to a house of former elegance

with a small dining room, tables set looking
a little tacky, barely enough chairs. I had to squeeze
one into no space at her table for myself.

I worried about her loose capris and t-shirt,
but in truth she didn't need me anymore. So, I sought
someone I'd have more in common with, spotting

an old friend who was oblivious to everyone
or perhaps seeing only what she could see looking
down as she stitched a tapestry.

I like the way you carried the old woman in your arms.
It was the right thing to do, the only thing. In your
Milky Way mind, dense with orbiting spheres and stars,

you didn't try to translate her fallen body into language
but simply, gently, lifted her, just as zoo gorillas
have done several times lately when a curious child

drops in. With grim nobility they raise the child,
their gentleness unhinged by onlookers' screams.
Woe can begin when the world responds.

TRAPPED IN THE MIRROR

The moment my father died, Walter,
nurse's aide extraordinaire, threw a sheet
over the mirror. This was my first experience

with covering mirrors in a house of death.
My father died in a Jewish nursing home,
we are Jews, Walter wasn't a Jew,

but like a zealous convert, he made sure
my father's spirit wouldn't be distracted
in its drift from a body ravaged

by uremic poisoning. The night before,
my father waved to his sisters summoning
him from the mirror across from his bed.

It was good that Walter covered the mirror.
That way we didn't have to see our disheveled
selves sitting with my father's corpse.

We should have turned his photographs
to the wall too, so he could quit his long life
without unappeasable yearning.

Of the many kinds of death, mirrors are
implicated in some. Fear of seeing oneself
reflected with the dead, some say, can kill.

It's an old, a far-flung custom, this draping
of mirrors, even portraits, in a house of death.
White gauze shrouded Abe Lincoln's mirrors,

black ribbons his portraits. Does this mean
Lincoln was a Jew? At the college where I taught,
we covered the art with white paper one day

each year to grieve artists lost to AIDS and
to fight for a cure. Some cultures invert mirrors
after death, but wouldn't the image right itself?

How mysterious, this intersection of death
with mirrors, portals to another world,
as Lewis Carroll and Jean Cocteau knew.

If a mirror is not draped after a death,
opportunistic spirits seeking to fill the void
can slip through it into our fragile world.

Even God loses strength when someone
created in and thus reflective of His image
dies. A corpse's reflection softens the seal,

sets loose malign forces. This and more
we must consider, such as how grief can cause
entrapment in the mirror, a particular risk

for people who have known much death,
sometimes mourning their own murdered
when proper burial wasn't allowed.

They see the faces of the dead hovering
with their own when they gaze into the mirror.
The more death, the more voids,

the more opportunities for mal-intentioned
spirits to emerge. This is how the living
end up trapped with the dead in the mirror.

Or the living may wander, empty inside,
exposed to specious notions, like thinking
that their suffering is unique. This converts

compassion to fear, and from fear, it's a short
step to hate: the blunting of the heart's proclivity
to experience the agony of others as our own.

When Dreams Begin Responsibility

It is both chilling and exhilarating
to open a door you never noticed before
and step into an unanticipated corridor,
a wing of rooms with open doors!

They are part of the house, were here
all the time! They're furnished! By whom?
Arranged with taste, the curtains, blinds,
the rugs and bedspreads, dressers, lamps,

by hands with rings, with a color of skin,
by faces crowned by a texture of hair; by people
who could be your cousins, who look and sound
and have a quirky gallows sense of humor like you.

The bathtubs and faucets are gleaming and cold.
Now your family can spread out, take all
the space they need. You can host your relatives
from up north! No closets? The rooms themselves

are closets, for they harbor evidence of hidden lives.
How strange that others were living here
while you pursued life on the wall's other side.
Were they expelled? But by whom?

This wing is part of your house, so you cannot
be a usurper. But if you're not, then why has
conscience carved a door? Why do you suddenly
see what you could not see before?

Like a citizen of the Reich moved into
a Jewish home to sleep on a Jewish bed,
fress at a Jewish table, find *tchotchkes* left
behind in corners of the Jewish floor,

you suddenly crave strong drink. Drink up!
You're living now where others lived before.
Drink up! Forget that they resided where you are!
Anything can pass from hand to hand, even mortar and land.

The house is yours. "Its reach and memory are long,"
so says this corridor of rooms. "That doesn't matter,"
so proclaims the relativity of law, the deed.
All such flightless wings are yours.

SLOW LEARNING

At last I could stop peeing on the way home,
soaking my socks and staining the new concrete
of 1950s America, for I had finally learned
which bathroom was which. This was the beginning
of my acclimation to life at school. I was five,
my hair cut Buster Brown, straight with bangs
the way I wear it now, though my Shadow doesn't,
she who was born the same year as I and whose name
is *Israel*. I watch her from the corner of my eye;
I witness her behavior through water. My Shadow
thinks her fear, self-love, and rage excuse her.
But nothing excuses anyone. I lied once
after peeing behind the rack of hooks at school
when a child who came to claim his little coat
saw the puddle stretching to a yellow star,
my own, and asked me quietly if I knew whose.

Middle East Shadow

When my hair waves,
my heart divides.
Once, with long hair,
straight and black as obsidian,
I was *Aviva*, wandering
up and down the wall, tasting
new words condensing on my tongue,
or sharpening my saber
on the wall's rough stone.
I loved to dash without fear
through Jerusalem streets,
always ahead of my shadow, forcing
the gravel to fly up behind me.
I admired the New lying on the Old
like sun on a rock, and savored
the Hebrew caress on the signs.
But when my hair masses
thick at the sides of my face
I am Fatima, drawn deep,
deep, into the cleft of history.
Within me the old maps are etched;
they honor my house and my orchard.
I teach them to my children
who pace that other world hovering
behind the new in smoky coincidence.
I open my hand: olives rest in my palm.
But they vanish, just beyond taste.

MOOSA

Moses had something to do with it,
ambivalent inheritor after Abraham begat
dual wicks that lit the Middle Eastern world.
Flash forward to me in an office crowded with books.
Here comes my one o'clock tutee, Moosa, Arabic
for *Moses*. His nose wrinkles when he smiles
like my childhood friend Rochelle's *yiddishe* grandmother's.
He's from Oman, and besides being hearing impaired
is dyslexic, so English is a challenge. Yet he narrates
nicely a photo essay about his country along with
some juvenile escapades, then, after prying from me
what I am, describes the tomb of an enormous Jew
whom pilgrims march around. At semester's end
Moosa says to me, "Come to Oman, bring the family,"
and I, bemused because of travel restrictions on Jews,
hear, "come to Paradise and bring the family,"
where hospitality rains and reigns because God
doesn't give a damn who's who.

TOO MUCH MATZO

Passover, 2014, the year
the gears of my Jewish heart
shifted. Dinner. Family.
Six boxes of matzo
bundled in cellophane.
Ascetic husband saying
you bought too much. He's right.
But it has no sodium, I say,
apropos of nothing. I read
the *Haggadah* in the bathtub.
Sacrilege? *Today we are here
but hope to be, next year, in
Jerusalem*. I wash my hair.
Attachment to the clay God
used to fashion Adam, then
bequeathed to his *begats*, to
Abraham, then sons and daughters
ramifying down generations
unable to imagine sharing it
is causing so much grief.
No wine, no ritual. Kids, nephew,
sister come just in time to eat.
Yes, there's meat and vegetables,
but the *fressing* focuses this year
on the bread of affliction: matzo
and *charoset*: mortar for walls,
matzo and butter, matzo ball soup.
I remember my mother's *kneydlekh*:
so hard we called them cannon balls.

CALL ME ISHMAEL

although it's not my name.
But call me Ishmael because
my porous borders can't make
rigid who I am. I could be him,
I must be, for I feel the justice
of his claim. Call me Ishmael,
for when it's all too much,
my hands are prone to disappear,
then float past as my cousin's hands,
"raised against the world." Call
me Ishmael because I had
black hair, because my skin
still darkens in the universally
endowing sun, Ishmael because
I crave the meals descendants
of his mother Hagar lovingly
prepare, Ishmael because
I can't accept the favoritism
of the Patriarch, its legacy
of blindness to injustice
passing now. Call me Ishmael
because I too wear sandals,
roam Judean hills, eat olives,
pasture sheep, and hear their
singing wool. His camels
carry me over the moon. Call
me Ishmael because I seek
my brother who was spilled
before being born. Where is he
in this world so wide of ours? I
find him in my cousin's home.

THEY THOUGHT OUR SINS WERE BREAD

The geese came gliding, each one carving a V on the quiet river,
toward our *Tashlich* service for *Rosh Hashanah* with its plea to God
to carry our sins to the sea. We stood on the banks of the Olentangy,
"river of red face paint" in the Seneca language, so misnamed
by legislators unaware that it was the Delaware who lived here
and had named it for the flint along the shore, *keenhongsheconsepung*,
literally "stone for your knife stream." These lakes and rivers
swelled with tears when tribes were marched out of Ohio,
which actually *is* Seneca: *ohi:yo'* meaning *great river* or *large creek*.
Indian names abound here like arias of absence. Never doubt
that absence has a song. Geese are more lovely on the water
than milling about. In flight, they form one *V*. Their honks
of warning, exultation, benediction are avian *shofars*
whose calls descend to us who must appear small from on high
though our feet leave prints deep and wide, sometimes
of damage, sometimes love. Water and sky: we traverse
but don't dwell in them. Lands where we'll never be warmed
by early inhabitants' flames. My people are not the only ones
by far who have suffered trauma, then inflicted trauma in return.
But because they *are* my people, I came to the river with Muslims,
Christians, and Jews: all accidents of birth: we enter the world
to find one another and try to stop tears. When I was nineteen,
I read the *King James Bible*. I was a virgin until one line penetrated me:
do not vex the stranger nor oppress him, for you were strangers in the land of Egypt.
Columbus, Ohio is no Egypt, having neither golden camels,
much to my dismay, nor golden sand. Columbus has, in fact,
much mud from weeks of rain. No one should be called a *stranger* here,
except, perhaps, by the geese, who saw us casting bits of bark,
understudies for our sins, upon the swollen river, so came gliding
with intersecting *Vs* to taste our bitter bread as if they were God.

DUCKS

In the alley near the railroad tracks I come upon
two ducks so slurried in sludge they are immobile.

For a moment I feel terrified someone poured thinned
cement on them, a vision of such breathtaking evil

it stops my heart. I wonder if I should carry them home
one by one for baths, fetch my car so they can stay together,

or call the wildlife folks. No rain is falling, though mercifully
the oven sun is cooling inside clouds. Full disclosure:

I wake, heart pounding, unable to exit this dream.
I tamp down the terror by turning on a light, picking

up a book, it happens *The Book of Joy*, and opening it
to where I left the Dalai Lama and Desmond Tutu in the last

of their leaves discussing *dukkah*, *suffering* in Buddhism,
hence *ducks* in the punitentiary of my dream. I think of

my own troubles, those of friends and family, the world's,
the burdens of these two men who manage nevertheless

to laugh together, one exiled but keeping spirits aloft,
the other ill but persevering. For me it's a quick quack

to the anguish of Palestinians and Jews, their destinies cemented
by Abraham, their souls slurried by *Nakba* and *Holocaust*,

their bodies magnetized to Middle Eastern soil,
their ears smothered by feathers that muffle the wind.

I want them to listen to the truths of each other's traumas,
to see shared blood in their faces, foods, intensity of mourning,

in their struggle for, against, the fickle Father's love.
Then they need to reconcile. For the ducklings' sakes.

They Tell Me My Grandfather

What is hateful to you, do not do to your neighbor: that is the whole Torah;
the rest is commentary.

Rabbi Hillel, when asked to recite the Torah while standing
on one foot.

They tell me my grandfather was arrested
for threatening a woman who was beating her child
on a street in Russia two century-turns ago.
He told her that if he saw her doing it again, he'd beat *her*.
Contrary to Russian literary tradition, the victim was not a horse.
In this way he launched the spanking prohibition in the family
that my mother, his daughter, adhered to.
On yearly visits to her family in Winnipeg, *mishpucha*
called my sister and me the *Katzenjammer Kids*.
My father, also a confirmed non-spanker, lost it
only once, taking off his belt to tenderize our bums,
but my mother stopped him, not unlike the way
my sister and I would thrust our little bodies between them
when they tried to dance. But that is another story.

They tell me my grandfather would sneak home
from the Russian army where he was a cook to sleep
with my grandmother, then creep back to his post
when the sun's fingers tickled the sky pink. No wonder
she had thirteen pregnancies, nine live births. My grandfather
hated the Russian army that Jews had a long tradition
of walking away from, especially if they lacked talent
on the violin, the only known path to deferment.
Ultimately, he didn't return to his post to stir the soup
but walked all the way to Winnipeg, secured a homestead,
sent for the wife and five extant kids. Quarantined in Liverpool
minus her sea-faring trunk, my grandmother washed
their only clothes at night, by day took them sightseeing
on a bus. That too is another story.

They tell me my grandfather, a religious Jew, "almost
a Rabbi," they say, gave Christmas gifts to Auntie Jean,
the Italian Catholic girl from Cicero who married his son Meyer.

O.K., so my grandfather was a religious man who kept kosher,
went to shul, studied the Torah, the Talmud, and, I'm guessing,
the Kabballah too. More to the point, he was a scholar
of the human heart. He knew that in Winnipeg, far from Cicero,
Jean would feel homesick on Christmas. Having mastered
the art of reciting the Torah while standing on one foot,
he knew how to bend and sway. I like that my grandfather
gave Jean presents on Christmas. The God I believe in
also approves. And that *is* the story.

III.

Sunday School

MIRACLE OF THE MASS

Because I sometimes find myself in churches,
I look around, wondering who else might be a Jew.
Usually I pick the very old because we steep
into shapes universally human. Muslim visitors
might imagine female congregants in veils, for
dressing others like ourselves helps us love them.
Once I saw a confused Protestant at a Mass
walk down the aisle to take communion.
She slipped the host into her purse. I smiled,
nudging my friend, who was both Catholic
and not amused. "Now," she said, "the Body
of Christ is trapped in that purse." But for me,
in that instant, the Miracle of the Mass came alive:
God, in humble transport, goes out into the world.

JEWS

If you saw them with their dark hair
and high-boned faces, you might call
these brothers *Jews*, but for the crucifix
above the doorway in the living room.
You might say *Jews* anyway, or *Job*
because there's trouble here, the cross
a steel abstraction glowing as if lit
from within, the blinds closed against day.
Here again, a mother and a son,
a mother and sons, but she without
the means to save them. Twice she
appeared to me in dreams, her skin
shedding light like a fish leaping,
water splashing from silver scales.
I need a Shaman to explain the symbolism
of those dreams: her whole body shining
amid dogs and cats, broken ceiling,
hobbled stove. The cross has no body
or face, for the man came down to walk
these rooms; men came down from
that high wall. Now two remain though
two are gone: the father and one son.

A FUNERAL

An old Jewish man attends a funeral mass
for a Catholic friend. They came of age together,
like vegetables and meat chunks in a stew,
went from marbles to pool to the track,
mixing up their skill with fate
until old age prevented it.
They never spoke of shul or church,
so when the old man sees his friend's obituary,
he writes the address on a scrap of paper,
pockets it, and takes a bus.

He's never been inside a Catholic Church.
He thinks the kneeling boards are for his feet.
He gazes up and up. He likes
the vaulted ceiling and the buttresses.
His little shul is more compact.
He likes the way he feels embraced in it.

The casket with his friend inside is open
so he waves good-by, not that he wants.
For death itself, his friend's, his own,
he doesn't weep. What makes him sad
is the Jewboy on the cross. How much
that must have hurt! And the poor mother!
And the pictures of his last hard walk!
A man so young, so handsome, in his prime—
he should have been out running on the beach,
or dancing with the girls, or playing cards
with buddies at a table squeezed
between the fridge and kitchen sink.

BREAD

I believe there is a battle between/the kitchen table, bimah, and altar.
The kitchen table/that serves food to hungry strangers wins.
Stanley Moss, "The Table"

It's old. It's us. It's everything, which is why
I'm baffled by the current gastronomic
turning away. Braided challah lit by candle flames.
Yeast dough rising, breathing on the board.
Incarnations of bread, nuances, iterations.
And bread's many noodle cousins!

These are my thoughts at a funeral mass
for the father of a student I taught twenty-five
years ago and whom I may not recognize today,
though we stayed in touch after he thanked me
by postal mail for ruining his chances for a lucrative career

by turning him on to writing. His father was a pathologist;
my son is a pathologist and artist whose mother
writes poems. Life, you wag, you lover of irony.

From a pew at Saint Andrew's, I'm comparing
the synagogue's bimah whose ark houses the Torah,
heavy bread for the soul, to something kindred here:
an altar with a cupboard holding a place setting
for the stupendously metaphorical small meal
served at Mass: cup, plates, tiny breads.

I watch the specifically baptized descend the slope
of the aisle to taste of it, some parting their lips
for the Priest to place the wafer on their tongues,
some taking it into their own hands, thinking,
as they ascend—I'm speculating now—of daily bread,
of trespass and forgiveness, of thorns and the salt of tears,
or of ordinary things, like mass produced bread
that nevertheless infuses the distracted air
around the factory with its tantalizing aroma.

Suddenly I remember the boy I loved in second grade
mesmerizing our class with a tale of loaves,
his father a worker in the bread factory
who took his son to see how they are made,
then sent down chutes to be wrapped in paper.
My classmate's arms are animated, his face glowing
as he shares the wonder we hunger for, his friends, his strangers.

SONG OF THE SHIELD

in memory of Sanikqua Hester

On the last day we were both alive
we made ourselves some salad, watched TV.
We smiled at folks we knew and didn't know,
wore sandals and cotton dresses open at the neck,
drank iced tea, then drifted, nudged
by heated hours, to our front porches,
where we sat up late talking with teenagers.

Wherever you were, the night was lovely beyond hope.
On branches of the catatonic trees, sparrows sang of falls
while streetlights burnished leaves, obscuring
the heroic tales of constellations, diverting eyes,
to their demise, to tales of the streets.

The last night we were both alive offered barely a breeze,
but somewhere a butterfly waved its wings,
landing on a lily, and after, someone driving by
sprayed her porch with bullets,

so that faster than thought, she took all she had—
all any of us has despite what we acquire—
and hushed her body begging to be saved
to wrap herself around the young male target
until all her cells were singing the song of the shield.

When I Opened the Door

Polished by the oils of many hands,
the oak door swung wide to a ram,

horns dripping leaves and twigs,
head low, snorting, smelling of figs,

confused and quaking in his wool,
bleating on the porch, dripping drool,

arriving fresh from his narration
obsessing on his flight, its repercussions.

Would Abraham, deprived of him,
seize on Isaac once again?

Then must the *Torah* be again composed,
and commentary, like a whole new forest, grow?

Was the ram a hero like the cow who flew
beyond the stockyard fence onto the evening news?

Or was his flight a curving horn,
theology a thicket denser than the mountain one?

SUNDAY SCHOOL

A Sabbath drawing in the Jewish press
of candles, wine, a braided loaf

makes me recall a synagogue parking lot
where my sister and I fought over the radio dial
while our dad was inside signing us up
for Sunday school, something my sister dreaded
but I begged for: the religious education
my friends were receiving.

I wanted to walk with shepherds on hills,
wave a curved staff at sheep as the sun slides,
hear God's voice in old wind. I longed to climb
the ladder in the prophet's dream.

I suspected there was more to life than
the playground cinders, or rather
something in the sparks we strike.

My dad returned to the car satisfied.
He had done his duty yet been spared
the hassle and expense: the classes
were full, he said, and I believed him.
So miscarried my religious education.
I was condemned to secular days.

I wanted in at the door.
It took me years to learn
it's a door-less door.

Why Does Abie Kiss the Church?

Why does Abie kiss the Church?
Because his friends insist. His books too,
loosely strapped, ho-humming by the fence,
especially the Latin that he hates.

Today he was a card in class, and cute.
They like him, how he jumps and grins each time
the ruler smacks the hands he can't subdue—
talking with one's hands is

forbidden by the rules. His pals make mischief too,
but they have curtained booths and priests
to intercede. He wrestles with himself
'til once a year the calendar his people tuck away

gives him a share. Like theirs, atonement has a river,
in his case Maine's Kennebec where his father,
having gone to the wrong Waterville
broke, alone, and lonely, almost threw himself.

From school they pass the Church. A breeze
is blowing, God's ubiquitous breath.
His fellows feel amiss, blame Abie,
peddler's son, who shares his people's
fringy faith. They tell him, "Kiss the Church."

Between his home and here, this edifice.
The stone feels cool, tastes sweet.
Inside, the mother, her Mizrahi Son,
the saints, the holy wafers, wait.

CHRISTINE ON THE DAYS OF AWE

The new wing, a *T* on the school,
had space for a piano to accompany
the sixth-grade chorus singing Christmas carols.
Never mind that out of every thirty kids per class,

one was not a Jew. My room's was Christine,
tardy every day, blond hair rolled, dress
pressed stiff, feet in ankle socks and pumps,
a little churchy for school but Dinah Shore pretty.

She yawned a lot, detached from all of us darker
nervous kids who sassed in ways she wasn't used.

Christine sits alone in class on the Days of Awe,
grinding pencils to slow points, removing
her shoes and socks to run her toes through
imaginary sand, rummaging in her desk

for paper. She writes a message, corks it
in a bottle, and sends it to drift on the sea
rising between rows of unoccupied desks.

THE DEMIURGE'S BOTCH

Either the cat punted it,
making a deranged field goal,
or the struggle inside skittered
the sticky trap across the floor,
so when I stumbled, dreaming, to the fridge,
I got a breakfast conundrum as profound as Job's.

I stooped to pick it up and screamed to see
a face, fur, pulse, then dropped it fast.

Unable to do nothing, though, I made
myself examine the mouse: badly stuck
yet so ambitious for life he was
trying to abandon his foot.

On the front steps, with butter knife and tears,
I opened up the charnel house, poured
warm suds, and worked dull silver
underneath the mouse until it scurried off
dragging its expendable pink and kindred toes.

All the while our cat gazed, robin-sung
and bored, in pleasant light.
"Shall I howl?" I asked myself.
I answered, "yes."

Do the Right Thing

The night before the march on the Statehouse
to encourage Ohio's electors to climb a mountain
of reason, I had a dream.

I was sitting in a circle of film buffs with Spike Lee!
He asked if anyone had something to say. "I do! I do!"
I cried, waving my hand,

then was off to the races, unable to restrain my flow
on beloved films from all over the world, my words
pouring from such depths

they fairly echoed. Which films? What did I say
about them? Nothing remains, only the felt intensity,
joined to the suspicion

that I was talking too much and would benefit
more from listening, in addition to Lee's patient
countenance as he turned

halfway away to gaze into the distance. Similarly,
decades ago, I found myself seated at a small round
table with W. H. Auden

soon after I began to write again. In that Dick Cavett
setting we talked poetics and poems all night,
the bliss of it remaining

though our words dissolved the moment I awoke.
In both dreams my soul was rent, my words were water
streaming from a gouged glass.

Two hundred of us marched around the Ohio Statehouse
on the nineteenth of December 2016, a bright cold day,
mostly in a loop

before the east façade, the side the sun rises on,
the direction Jews gravitate to in cities, and Muslims
kneel to worship God,

and where the hoped-for Hamilton electors would enter
while marchers with bullhorns led us in rhymed chants
ending with "do

the right thing," cameras recording us, the telltale
lambs' wool top-coats of the powerful darkly swaying.
For them, the "right thing"

was mistaken for the wrong thing, the thing we were there
to prevent in this bitterly ironic age, for the electors failed
to apprehend the spirit

of civic duty. The lessons of great films and poems might
have cracked open the seals on their hearts, which may
be why Lee and Auden

let this novitiate yack the night away, Auden, who revealed
our mortar of Eros and of dust, its urgent flame,
and Lee, who

embedded an imperative phrase into the culture,
one the electors didn't know to know, so kicked
it away like a can.

MATTER AND SPIRIT MOVE ON DIFFERENT PLANES

By the time our eight-year-old son's red nylon jacket
arrived with his name embroidered on it, he had
already quit the Columbus Boy Choir. Matter must
move fast to keep pace with spirit. While he was a member,
they sang at the State Auto nativity scene downtown,
the statues now arranged in side-park dioramas
to tell the story—life-sized angels, shepherds, wise-men,
camels, sheep, goats, a dog, an ox, and a husband with his
destiny-swept pregnant teenage wife waiting for the baby
to be hand-delivered by a local child on Christmas eve.
Everything is *a cappella* sung and lit from below, light
aspiring, the whole display like solid Technicolor shadows
of events from long ago, matter chasing spirit,
in this case across millennia. When a soft drizzle
thins the crowd, we leave to get some dinner.
Returning to the car we meet a man who says
he hasn't eaten for days and who truly seems to be
hovering between flesh and spirit—ill or doped or mad
or starving—how can one tell? We give him a sandwich,
then drive away waving. He waves back, chewing
a bite of it. He looks as if he's shambling after its box,
for he is holding it before him, but really it is the box
that is shambling after him. The sky clears. High clouds
drift. Stars wink from a far distance, their gumptious
dust so energizing that our eyes will have to be
weighted to sleep by the Sandman's sand. No matter
what, and wherever they may be, the souls of the just
are likewise running ahead of the bodies that breathe them,
out of sync and propulsive, lighting, not torching, the world.

SAINT KITCHEN

Now that the back porch is down, light floods the kitchen,
falling on the table, skimming bowls of tomatoes and fruit,
anointing the glass doors of the cabinet, penetrating
to its dishes, cups, plates, and the many bowls I keep buying
because they are vessels. Skillets rotate in the kitchen's heavens,
flashing radiance. The cherry counter slowly, coolly burns,
the breadbox and toaster glowing. The black and white tile
is slick with liquid light that waited over a hundred years
for welcome here. Spices, diaphanous with dust, dance
on the stove's ledge while the kettle sings. Some evenings, it's true,
light pours in through the dining room's stained-glass window,
the Beat Sun hastening West, to crown my husband's
stately head. But the demise of the porch has invited
this kitchen miracle, beatifying what lives and what is
brought to life by living hands. Light drenches my eyes,
kindling hope that even if I cease to see, I will still know its energy.
I remember leaning into it, growing toward it, as a child.

BLESSING THE SUN

God bless the amber soul of the morning sun
nudging twigs, nascent leaves, and blossoms
in bulbs and seeds, startling sub-rosa worms,

then lapping like a dog of light to this come-hither
wide east window to kindle the old cat
all the way to her orange bones as she leans

into it dozing. My own damp head sputters
with a word I don't know: *Hosannah!* for lit spindles
of high-backed empty chairs draped with drying laundry,

for the gilded newspaper in its throes,
and for the carpet's woven tigers and deer
leaping and spinning around their mandala.

My Dog's Church

We climb out of the wooded ravine, my dog and I,
near a small stone church. Instead of a cross,
a ship carved in stone sails above the arched door:

waves, salt air, adventure, fish, instead of agony.
My dog leaps up the steps with a spirit of entitlement,
never mind that by adoption he's a Jew,

and never mind we're landlocked here: sails
give our thoughts wind. On the lawn a sign proclaims
the days on which to donate food. My eyes

fill with tears, a universal reaction studies say
to human kindness, empirical proof of the soul.
It's water that connects us all, engenders and joins.

Trees, erect and fallen, commiserate with the creek
in the ravine all day, but the stone church is quiet
in the way that churches tend to be, an implosive hush

verging on song, vast and echoey as dogs, who, when
not barking, move their lips and stare, or on our legs
with secret creed of nosiness or zeal for a good scratch lean.

IV.

I Am Sitting at My Parents' Table

They Are Running to My Mother

My cousin Lela in Toronto tells me immigrants
are arriving in Canada minus fingers and toes.
Some are crossing frozen fields at relaxed
stretches along the border between North Dakota
and Manitoba, fleeing America like Eliza did
in *Uncle Tom's Cabin* from a related disease,
treading ice with her baby in her arms wrapped
in a shawl. Lela really called to see how Laura's
doing after back surgery, but we slip into Trump
talk inevitably. That was several days ago, though
these days are one long night. Tonight, after walking
under clouds spitting rain, small drops landing
on my cheeks like tears falling of their own volition,
the evening news shows me a Somali man kneeling
frostbitten, and parents rubbing their baby's tiny toes,
all finding refuge first in Emerson, Manitoba, then
in Winnipeg, having fled America, of all places,
with its Emma Lazarus scripture, to arrive in the dark
like dreams, or confessions rising from the unconscious
guilt of a nation. Today in Winnipeg it is minus 20°,
so cold you might wish to die when the wind blows,
where my mother was born in 1912, her refugee mother
giving birth to her alone on the farm, her refugee father
waiting to register her birth until May when he was
going to town anyway. Today Winnipeg's Salvation
Army is setting up beds in spare rooms, just as
my mother often did for *mishpocha* from Canada
after she became an American. Beyond the Bardo now,
my mother is so fused in my memory with Winnipeg
that it seems to me our refugees are running to my mother.

VISITATION

I dreamed my father came back
looking macerated, mostly a voice,
but unmistakably his timbre.
I asked him, "What's it like?"
He said, "You can forget about
the Big Man, but there are lots
of Lesser Authorities." This came
not, I am certain, from my head,
that believes in a Central Light
whose chief virtue is Unmyopic
Sanity, but was my father's
singular message to me,

or something, perhaps, from Cocteau.

Split Self

There are two sides/to any argument; //one arm/in each sleeve.
Rae Armantrout, "Control"

My father was a *schmatta* salesman, peddler
of stuff used to make pants and sleeves.

He looked at life through a dealing/promoting lens.
I, on another of so many hands,

read events like poems, their meanings rising
like steam the way meanings waft from metaphors.

Two sides? I spent my green years confident
we have unified selves. So I'd be confounded

by my own and others' contradictions.
Eventually I learned to acknowledge

the random rubble we as humans with
our smooth or rough façades, carry inside.

Sleeves remind me of our split, but also its corollary,
the bilateral symmetry we share with animals, birds,

even fish, our earliest grandparental exemplars.
Of course, two can be subdivided further,

like those ramified, leafing, flowering,
fruiting, waving, sometimes murdering,

more often murdered, reaching for
the heavens trees.

Rag Man's Sons

My father appeared as Kirk Douglas in my dream.
He did this to get my attention, says the woman at the dog park.

Sensing a compassionate listener, I confide in her
that my dog bit me, and that later, while walking him,

I begged my father, who passed away in '97, to help me train him.
That night I had the dream. But first, you need to know

my father loved dogs, other animals too, who loved him back.
When he was twelve, his cat gave birth to kittens in his bed

while he was sleeping. Kittens are, of course, another
kind of dream. In mine, I'm sitting on a folding chair

in a row of such chairs on a sunny Hollywood lot
when here comes Kirk Douglas in his prime,

a basket of vegetables, mostly purple onions, on his arm.
I smile and holler, "Hello Kirk Douglas!" He grins,

bends, kisses my cheek. I laugh too boisterously.
"You need to calm down," Kirk Douglas says to me.

It was one of those early morning dreams that seem
to come from somewhere beyond the self. How do I know

Kirk Douglas was a stand-in for my father? Because his admonition
matched my need, both he and my dad were rag men's sons,

and once I wrote a poem about my dad called "Onions."
The dog park woman's comment was the *afterword*.

Here's the *epilogue*: we kept the dog, forgive him often, love him.
We also splurged on consults with a behavioral veterinarian.

Have a *postscript* too: after I asked for his help, my dad
affixed his mustache to my dog's snout.

But when I gaze into his canine eyes, I see
my father's skepticism.

My Brother, Golem, Absconder

My sister invented you for strangers on the bus,
molded the waxwork of your olive face,
matured you fast, then sent you off to war,

your life and death exhaled between her frosted lips
before she sidled down the well of steps.

Or at bars, beneath a nest of ratted hair and squeezed
into a booth with some guy, she interposed you.

Plum of our parents' rapture, you'd have taught us
all about the shape of men. Your genius would have
multiplied our misbehaviors.

Instead you seized the moment, Mother bleeding
and the doctor drunk—or if my sister's dream is true,
our teenaged father's unacknowledged son

by some fey wisp in Waterville—to shirk
lugubrious life and slip away.

ODESSA POGROM

Her Ukrainian neighbor pulls her from the street
to hide her until the storm blows over. My grandmother
runs her fingers over the attic floorboards, tracing a dark history.
The trees asleep in the wood transport her to a forest
where she bends to pick mushrooms from cool earth,
then rises to taste berries in the brambles on the path.

She is not alone. A four-month child is turning in the waters of her womb,
plucking her veins like the strings of a harp, while the neighbor who shelters her
paces below, blonde hair straying from the braids around her face,
eyes wide with foreboding.

In the attic room, a little window blinks its dusty light too high
to show the street, so she only hears the hooves and curses,
steel and smothered sounds like sacks of rags and books
that fall from carts of drunkards whipping horses in the snow.

As the sea of sound rises the room takes off. She is belted to the mast;
the wails of stricken children are the shrieks of birds blown
sideways in the wind to crash against the waves.

On floors below, her neighbor presses her palms together,
holding the blood in.

SWEET BLOOD

Before there was insulin, or pills
to stimulate the pancreas,

before a finger could be pricked
at home or on the go to bleed a drop

onto a strip in a phone-sized meter,
making it sing like a stool pigeon

of the blood's alleged sweetness,
my diabetic grandma on my mother's side

had to weigh her food and was told
not to fast on *Yom Kippur*, that doing so

would be a kind of sacrilege, for
the need to maintain health

takes precedence over religious obligations
But fast this fleer of pogroms

to Manitoba's prairie, thirteen times
with child, of legendary kindness,

arms folded over heart to rest on
bountiful and sagging bosom, did.

I Am Sitting at My Parents' Table

I am sitting at my parents' table
having a lunch of a bagel with tea.
My father sits across from me,
drumming on the tablecloth.
He ate a meal at ten o'clock
and waits for a car to dialysis,
repeating this familiar line:
"That must be the way it is,"
responding to nothing I have said:
I'm silent sitting across from him.

You might say I'm struck dumb by his eyes,
magnified by cataracts,
the same deep sea green as his shirt,
by my little mother with curled white hair
who waits on me, for I see the pain
in the stiffness of her hips and knees,
and by light that pours through slatted blinds
on this first incontestable day of spring.

Mother joins us, drumming her fingers too,
and I want to utter a string of lies:
that I woke today a physician degreed
and discovered suddenly how to revive
my father's failed kidneys and how to anoint
my mother's arthritic joints.

My father takes his wallet out,
a ritual too, and begins to sort
through all the cards he has inside,
looking for something new to say,
some amazing fact about his life
with which to impress both me and himself.
But all he finds is a bordered card
from the funeral home where they have arranged
for their own cremations, and I feel ashamed.

MAVENS IN AN ENIGMATIC WORLD

In the era of long-playing records, you unpack your
first stereo, trying not to think less of your father
for asking why you bought *two* speakers. Who wouldn't
be a lousy Connecticut Yankee in King Arthur's Court?

~

Your parents suffer for a week the cricket
chirruping in their apartment before telling you
it is driving them insane. You drive there
to change the battery in their smoke alarm.

~

When your sister drinks from the garden hose,
your father delivers this memorable line:
"Stop! You'll blow your lips off!"
She envisions her lips sailing across the yard.

~

He also lends intrigue to biology when you tell
your sister to go suck an egg, and she plucks one from the carton,
puts it in her mouth. This time your father shouts,
"Don't do *that*! It comes from a chicken's *tuchus*!"

~

It turns out he was right.

PIGGY

My sister gave our mother the nickname *Piggy*
after finding her facing a kitchen corner, polishing off
a cream puff, whipped cream peaked on her nose.
The moniker stuck. A language evolved.

We called a tidy house *piggified*, a visit to our mom
pigging it, the plural form for Mom and Dad *the Pigs*;
Mom alone, *Piggy, Pink Pig, Pinkness, Hambone, Ham.*
Warnings of impending parental visits were *Pig alerts*.

Finding our mother well, we pronounced her *fork tender*.
The hospital that treated our parents was *Porksicordia*,
after Winnipeg's *Misericordia* where Mom's brothers
were doctors on the staff. The trope's wave crested,

leaving in its wake a plethora of objects: pig trivets,
coasters, hooks, and other pig-embellished gifts Mom
tucked away only to find them returned to the light of day,
put back on display by the two-headed monster, her daughters.

On a flight through Atlanta to a family reunion, my sister
said "Piggy" out loud. Exiting the plane, we heard
the stewardess mumbling to herself, "Pig-eye? Pig-eye?
I wouldn't want someone calling me Pig-eye!"

Complicating this, we're Jews, alleged shunners of pork,
admirers of pigs only from afar. Be assured, affronted reader,
that we never devoured our mother nor served her up on a platter
as in unhealthy love, though I admit we salted her some.

My Father Passing

For a week, my father's hands gestured like a pontiff's
as he whispered "please" and "please."

When he called my sister "wonderful" on his last lucid day
from his nursing home bed, my mother shoved me
forward for my share of his blessing.

In that beige box of a room, his mind replayed
a blizzard born of dementia created by his great toxicity.
Worse, a blizzard in a war. He begged us,
"bundle up and stay together."

The night before my father died, I pulled sweats
over flannel pajamas to drive through snow
for the vigil in his room.

Little veins were broken all over my father's face
from dying's labor. He was a begrimed miner
straining to lift his last shovelful of coal.

I touched my father's forehead, then made a nest
of everyone's coats behind a chair. So I hid
like a mole from the death of my sire.

I spent the night on that cold floor, clocked
by his dying rattle. At dawn, I went home to shower.
While I was gone, he passed. I returned to his corpse,
altered so imperceptibly that the Rabbi sat next to him
and casually conversed.

I haven't wept, unless you count the river of sorrow
for my father that drenched me in a dream.

MY FATHER ART IN HEAVEN

I am no child thrust up from some troubled love,
stamped with a father's swagger and wild eyes.
My father was as plain as salt, and I was given
time enough to sketch his grizzled face.

Near the end he would rise from bed, peering at us
around a corner. First, we'd see his eyes,
little sunlit Caribbeans, then his tufted head.
He would enter the room clubbing the floor with his walker,
his thick white mustache impeccably combed.

Now he sits on a chair at the Grand Racetrack,
his walker a trellis for vines. His hair is long and white,
like after he retired. He is wearing pants that look like jeans
but are made of polyester. I want to talk with him,
but he is poring over a racing form, his fingers
tracing horses like birds fluttering over a stable.

He worked away his life, a salesman *sans* the failure
and the dreams. Now he is spending eternity casting his lot
with sage horses, coins dripping like manna from their manes.

Their names have a revelatory slant: *Mad News, Transcendent Itch,
Shy Breed, Dancing Fool, Dutch Uncle.* But these he discounts,
nor does he heed the jockeys, the famed of them whom
nature cast to sit on striding thrones. Instead, he tips
his mild chin up to observe Heaven's weather, then notes
the track's condition and picks the horse most nimble on dust.

But when they line up at the gate and the gun blasts,
a surge compels his knees, and my father rises.
When the horses round the curve, wind blows him
into the realm of wonder, for *Afterlife's Mystery*
pulls ahead, on whom he made a modest bet.

Fiasco Under an Impeccable March Sky

Today I am trying to fetch my ninety-three-year-old mother
who is leaning on a cane, waiting for me near the back exit

of her doctor's office. But the city keeps rearranging its roads
until I end up in Gahanna, Hebrew, almost, for Hell.

There are many ways to reach the people you love,
but getting lost isn't one of them.

This fiasco unfolds like one of those dreams wherein you forget
to wear clothes, then streets and buildings pull a semblance bait-and-switch

until you can't get to where you're trying to go. In waking life,
a small distilled self stands to the side, watching, lifting a brow,

confident of resolution though curious about how before the Big
Kahuna of tomorrow washes the crisis away. Meanwhile,

it helps to have a cell phone and someone to call, in this case
a husband who has learned to filter hysteria to glean facts,

like the doctor's name. He looks up the number, but because
he isn't in the car, he doesn't get to hear hysteria's encore

when an office recording says they are closed for lunch,
though my sister must pour a cup of tea to contemplate

my Hindenburgian bulletins on her answering machine from I-670 East
and I-270 South, from Mock Road and sundry ravines between

describing how all my efforts to reach our mother are taking me
farther away, how roads, malls, suburbs, ramps, and intersections

are flinging themselves around until I suspect the revenge
of this former farmland: itchy oats, angry wheat, buried brome.

IDLY BY

I stood idly by, listening to our dying mother's
Vicodin hallucinations while my sister grew tall
from being cast as the cleaner of a by-gone stall

on the Kobrinsky dairy farm where she was sweeping up
a rainbow of chicken feathers. "What a good girl," our mother said,
while I played the usual ear, like when I stood idly by

all those years they cast their love as a brawl.
On Saturday, the day before our mother died,
I stood idly by, but this time prone, having crawled

onto her narrow bed to hold her. Most of me fit,
but part of me was balanced between the mattress and the wall,
my *tuchus* accidentally pressing the button to call

the nurse. In this way I gathered up the gleanings of her love
while the oxygen pump heaved its rendition of Hal,
making our mother's chest, like Lake Winnipeg, rise and fall.

I'd have breathed for her but couldn't. So I stood idly by
until I was ejected, hoven by the magnet of her mercy
from her room, down the long hall,

and through the exit. That is how I came to be standing idly by
elsewhere in the city while our mother, in death's thrall,
held my sister's heartbroken hand. Then came the call

and I was floating, separated from my mother's body,
a preposterously aging orphan with a grief only
the Mourner's *Kaddish* could release so I could bawl.

MOTHER LEAVES THE BARDO

I woke to see Mother sitting on a chair
by my bed. Just sitting there, not saying a word,
even when I asked, "why didn't you wake me?"

She was waiting for me to see her so she
could fade, having passed away years before.
Yet here she was again to say good-bye.

It seems that there are partings, other partings,
more. After her death, I dreamed her back, over
and over. Was I summoning her? Or was she

trying to return? Panic filled those dreams
the way flood water inundates low, then high ground.
Panic about renting her old apartment,

or the small flat I dreamed near the airport
in Winnipeg abutting departures, returns.
Panic about retrieving her furniture, shopping

for her food at the Main Street Kroger. But no.
She'd be too frail to cook. She'd have to return
to the nursing home where she'd been happy.

Why did we ever let her leave? Impossible now
to get her back in. And where was Father?
Gallivanting on business. Enough with his trips!

How, ten years older than she, one hundred
and sixteen if he's a day, can he still be driving
the circumference of his territory, managing

to be the eternal salesman? After each dream,
I woke knowing my parents were gone.
Father still visits in various ways. But Mother—

ever since the night I woke to see her sitting
next to my bed on a wooden chair she must have
schlepped with her from the Bardo, waiting patiently

for me to open my eyes in awareness of how
she was tending me still—left for her next
mysterious juncture, departing even my dreams.

Last Repast

Eternity sits in the empty chair.
An otherworldly light ignites
the table like a chandelier.
Mother stands in kitchen,
davening with a sponge.
Father sits at table nodding,
napkin under chin. Grandsons
flank him, set to right him if he leans.
Behold the patience of knives and forks,
the coyness of spoons, to feed a man
profoundly disinclined toward food.
Enter fools in the garb of matrons,
eyes winking from mirth and tears,
with carryout Chinese. Suddenly
his arms are Siva's whirring
in the soy and garlic steam,
stoking his mouth with egg rolls,
bok choy, chicken, thin slices of beef.

Let's Eat the Delicious Potatoes

for Mim

Let's eat the delicious potatoes with parsley, butter, and salt,
steamed in their skins. Eat them warm like the hearts
of asylum seekers, not out of cannibal proclivities but sympathy,
taking their travail into ourselves, potatoes as symbols,
for if not ours now, our forbears' then.

Sustaining is the privilege, the grace, of the endowed potato,
as many Irish knew, who were saved by them, and Van Gogh
also knew, immortalizing those who cultivated, ate, and grew
to resemble them. In truth, we all resemble potatoes, with
our earth-toned skins, our wrinkles and sprouts. With luck,
we will likewise be hardy, delicious, adaptable.

Films occasionally cameo potatoes. In a scene in Richardson's
The Loneliness of the Long Distance Runner, for example,
Colin and his beloved Audrey consider social class and vocation
while leaning on a wall—a wall, it bears repeating—eating chips
from newspaper cones to absorb the oil. Colin is struggling, unresolved.
We know of his hunger for justice and work-life satisfaction via potatoes.

One could do worse than be a potato, for if true beauty lies within,
then potatoes are beautiful. They pleasure the epicure, sustain the hungry.

My Aunt Mary used to say, "eat your potatoes" in her accent
to whomever was listening at dinner. I'm struck now
that she prioritized potatoes over meat and milk. I was all ears,
for I loved hearing her native Russian drag her English over stones,
or perhaps potatoes, a word she gave an unforgettable auditory reverb.
I must be imitating her more than I think, because today
my grandchild left a post-it on my laptop saying, "eat
your potatoes." I read it aloud in Aunt Mary's voice.

RAGGED FORMATIONS

in memory of Jimmy Cohen

Blue as the early morning sky, I am gazing
over the backyard fence with my dog when
honking from a ragged majesty of geese,
twenty or more souls in loose formation,
reel our eyes upward, our spirits in tow.

Flying far is hard, best done in flocks,
even if the form be raggedy.

My father's father, ghost to me, forced for future
to America, passed through Ellis Island,
then took a train to the wrong Waterville,
his ländsmen waiting for him in Waterville PA
as he rode, with the last of his shekels, to Waterville Maine.

A teenager alone with a peddler's sack on his back,
he couldn't sell a thing to save his soul. The murky
Kennebec River invited him in. *One more house
before I jump*, said his body. The housewife there
bought everything while Canadian geese
honked joyfully, almost home.

Brushes, string, cookpots, knives, patent medicines,
like poems, must pass to others, a difficult sell some days.
Do geese sweat with the labor of pulsing their wings
to stir and smooth the sky? Or is that ache
eased by their capacious view?

I think they're born and born again
in immersions that go by many names
each time they tunnel through misty clouds.

V.

Heart and Soul

Rounding the Edge of the World

We pumped the pedals of our Schwinns for several blocks,
leaning around corners to see the trees give way to saws
and tractors pull up stumps like teeth out of the mouth of earth.

We rode again to scattered chocolate holes, pretending
steam shovels scooping earth were invaders from *War of the Worlds*.

The next time we rode by the movement was toward air:
the flaked blue sky was framed by angled wood,
the open structures breathed with wind, and working men
who sweated in their plaid and swung their six-by-tens
ignored us as we darted in and out and found no bones.

Four months later when we rounded the edge of the world,
new houses were up, a new road paved and lined with curbs,
and the street given a name with *haven* in it.

Babble in the air told us refugees were moving in.
The sounds of their words bypassed our sense,
so we listened instead to the music of their eyes,
the surface of dark pianos flecked with light,
and to their dark hair humming in waves, proof that shaved,
a thick and heavy mass would grow back in.
Though Jews like them, we were more like Howdy Doody,
they like the deep dyed wool of Persian rugs, the braided fringe,
like emeralds and rubies, or stews thick with sour cream.
They didn't have much to move in: their sofas were webbed lounge chairs.
Yet they rubbed their hands together in a friction of disbelief:
now they were sprayed from the great showerhead of suburban American sun:
we and they were washed in light.

On the day we wanted popsicles but had no nickels,
we piled junk in a red wagon and trekked from door to door.
Nobody on our block wanted our buttons and screws,
old boots and square bottles filled with colored water,
but when we came to the street of refugees,

the women sidled down their steps wide-hipped
to poke two fingers through our heap and ask, "do you have th'read?"
They took us more seriously than we took ourselves,
so that even the razzing we got back at school—we'd been seen—
was quelled by a peddler's wonder.

One day, the *O* of hunger driving our limbs after swimming
all day at the local pool, we rode our bikes down the street of refugees
to stop at Irene's aunt's. At five o'clock her rooms were backlit
by the sun, the kitchen bathed in sleepy light, the Sabbath chickens
cooked and cooling on the counter. Need I say we fell upon
those chickens and picked bones clean before we pedaled home?

And now it's a street of the mind I ride, hosting its various weathers,
its flowers colored by immersion in the soul. On it I see
her aunt's surprised, not angry face, black numbers needled
on her arm, her silvery long earrings flicking, drinking light.
I hear an ocean turning in the ripples of her voice, and taste
those roasted peppered holy birds as I marvel too that I
was there to ride about at the creation of the world.

GIMLI, LAKE WINNIPEG

The sky over the lake was loafing blue,
the water teased the shore and made the pines
look just like men who'd rolled their pants
to flee around the shoreline bend
where dark clouds gathered out of view.

Daddy pulled the Ford into the alley
behind Uncle Louie's cottage to the sound
of the lake's glub, the cadence of wind,
and the next door little blond boy's greeting,
"I don't like you! You have blawck hair!"
Giddy after days of driving, we laughed
and made friends.

By afternoon the heat drove us all into the lake—
even the neighbor's mutt waded in to bite the water.
Only Aunt Wilma didn't swim but remained at her easel,
painting the landscape, giving the motionless lake
fierce white caps, the girly lake that in ten years
would pull her husband to its heart and ravish him,
fling back his wool-clad body with a ticking watch.
On this day, though, he's fixed like a photograph,
arms churning the water, knighted by blades of sun.

At dinner, little cousin Nora in her highchair
rewarded all our coaching by lifting her baby brow
to nonchalantly say, "Daddy, you're a bitch."
He kept on carving the roast. When Auntie Rose
told handsome cousin Peter to take a girl out
for a roll behind a bush to cure his acne, we loved
the clacking of tongues, dinner's rapid decline,
then after, how the grown-ups lolled on chairs
in the screened-in porch, talking, smoke from
Aunt Bella's cigarette coiling, thinning toward the light.

We skipped out to the music of Canadian vowels
slipping back into Mommy's speech
to join the cousins in the yard rearranging fish-flies
on the screens, unhooking their legs
and launching them like tiny planes.

At night, my sister and I put to bed in the white cabin,
I lay in the dark still feeling the ripples of sand
on the floor of the lake. As I waded more deeply
into sleep, fish-flies gathering again on the screen,
I saw Aunt Mary, once a milkmaid girl with long black braids,
almost a widow now, standing in the water,
her breasts floating on the surface of the lake.
She curved her back to bathe her arms,
splashed water on her freckled chest, and murmured,
"Oy, it's a *mechaieh*," blessing us all in the parted waters.

LOOK AT THE SEA

The blocks were gridded rows,
      rigid like the times. Yet Miramar curved
          its way through order, all the way
             from Mayfield Road to Green, winding like
                a path for cows through farms now sub-
             divided into lots with modest homes raised up
         on ground a little higher than the inner city's.
      Dads were veterans then, or refugees, and moms
wore aprons tied in back with bows to cook and keep
      the fruit bowls full for sons who sidled onto stoops
         with lipstick Ss on their shirts, slugging down quarts
            of milk, and for their daughters who were ticking.
               We could see the country club a block and boulevard
             away from Miramar, its lush golf course perpetually
         green. It was restricted against Jews. Yet somehow,
    who knows how? it wounded in a way that kept us busy
liking who we were. So when the rain came down so hard
      the sewers overflowed, and Miramar became a sea, we
         kicked off shoes to splash and dance in it, deluded we
            were wealthy, loved beyond compare, and had it all.

ONE RAIN

In my ninth year
in a heavy summer rain
we pulled boots over bare feet
to play in the downpour. It was
one of those luxuries of childhood,
letting your clothing, skin, and hair
get soaked, lifting your face to
the extravagance of a beneficent
summer storm. The drops, tiny
softened crystals, fell from great
elusive chandeliers, and Irene,
our friend with thick dark curls
that my mother would run her
fingers through *kvelling*, Irene
whose house hosted relatives with
exotic names like *Unda* and *Simmy*,
and boarders, and whose mother
bore black numbers on the soft
white skin of her arm—Irene
bested our stomping in puddles
by flinging herself into the river
extemporized on the downslope
to the corner, rolling and laughing
on the glistening carless street.

PLAY

Act I

They sing out "Norman Google-eyes,"
trying to tease him from his silent house,
hoping he will step out on the porch for scrutiny
on a partly sunny, robbed of revelation April day.
They ring his doorbell, run away, repeat, believing
they are masters of a magic strong enough to make
a grown man living with his parents on account of
secret suffering appear. Their mischief rakes his
hands through his hair, shuffles his gait, then opens
his vest, revealing a wrinkled shirt through which
their ignorant but curious Superman-inflected
x-ray eyes might see his heart, scattershot artillery
twanging in his chest. Like a cut beet, it will
stain whoever stretches out a palm and touches it.

Act II

Disappointed he does not appear, they go home
for a game of Monopoly to consume the afternoon.
But Norman, weary of derision, leaves his house,
ambles up the street, and pauses at the very door
behind which they are venturing, a banker chosen,
cash doled out. The graphics of the game: its color-coded
class-inflected properties, iconic rich man twirling cane,
its fateful cards, repeating circuits tread with selves
reduced to iron, thimble, canon, Scottie dog; in short,
the game's bald metaphors cannot compete, are always
second best to probing Norman's mysterious heart.
Unaware he knows both who and where they are,
they have their turn to jump when the doorbell rings.
It feels a little cutthroat, like the game.

Act III

An indulgent mother answers the door while
they scuttle the board, all they have amassed
or lost, to lurk so as to better hear when Norman
asks, soft-spoken, dignified, for the taunting to cease.
As well he must, for each year following the rupture
of the war, the quasi-healing of the peace, more children,
energized excessively by life propelled from tragedy,
appear on the block. The mother, who defends them
fiercely even when they're wrong, avoids Norman's eyes,
so utterly misprized in the shallows of their lexicon.
His anguish, shock, intelligence, it's true, have made
them bulge, but his are eyes that whosoever purchases
increasing depths of spirit with the shekels
that experience pays will grow to have.

Nimbus

She leans on the steering wheel, face framed by black waves,
soul scarred by barbed wire. She considers shoes, groceries,
a color of paint, but beneath these musings, prisoners with parcels
line up to enter trains, and cheering peasants show no mercy.

Four twelve-year-olds bounce in the back seat, I among them
with pajamas, toothbrushes, clean underwear, on our way
to the slumber party of a friend who has recently moved
to a huge old house in a wealthy suburb. When we tell
the mother driving us her name, she hits the brakes.
Had she known the family was German, she
never would have taken us! We are stunned.

~

After exploring our friend's mansion via winding stairs,
we settle in a dim-lit corner of the living room to work our magic,
placing each one of us two fingers under our seated friend,
chanting *she's as light as a feather* until she flies up weightless,
as high as our young arms can reach. She's so bright,
an angel, the lamp haloing her yellow hair, emblazoning
the shadow of her thin frame on the wall.

Breakfast Ago

Girls saunter in the predawn mist,
gathering one another for a trek
before the sun, wagon filled

with morning food, not refugees
on a dusty road laden with belongings,
but Jewish off-white suburb girls

trekking to a park because someone
said *let's have a breakfast picnic,*
probably Rochelle.

They make a pyramid of coals, squirt
lighter fluid on, toss in a match, watch
fire flare, wait for the crimson glow

with ashen edges signifying they are
hot enough to cook on, so familiar now.
I'm there, laying bacon in an iron pan,

cracking eggs to sizzle in the grease,
toasting bread directly on the flames,
setting plates, and pouring juice.

We eat. The sun has risen. Robins sing.
The park is empty but for us, who staked a claim.
In coming years, we learn to dance, some well,

pair off with boys, forget our bond. Sheila,
caelia, heaven, is the first to go. I'm trying
to sieve the essence of that day, now gazing

down with aerial shots and tracking shots,
but I can't hear what we say, pre-teen,
pre-binary, chasing the dark away,

then pulling the almost empty wagon home.
We heard the culture's clamor faintly,
knew of terror once removed, then

caged and locked in history, hid troubles,
lacking words. We raided our parents'
larders with impunity and knew not want.

BEAUTY

Her last name was the formal version
of a common male nickname. Biblical too.
Never mind what. Suffice to say that she
was beautiful. I wanted to be like her,
the way she stood aloof from the snorting herd
in the junior high hallway, her brown hair
waving how I wanted my straight hair to wave,
her white blouse tucked into a waist cinched small.
I cinched mine too, though I, a chatterbox,
could never imitate her serene style.
Add this exotic fact: she was but half a Jew.
I longed to straddle worlds like her, dip genes
·from a wider pool, know other gods, confuse
the populace, and claim as my people the world's.

SWIMMING WITH MARGIE ON AND OFF THE ROAD TO HEAVEN

We stayed awake all night goofing around
while Margie's parents slept, her mother

racked by Shoah dreams, her father,
a survivor too, but magical, the builder of

a six-bedroom house with double-winding stairs,
hand-painted flowers in the hall, wall-to wall

shag carpeting, a walk-in fridge, and an outdoor
in-ground pool where Margie and I swam naked

under a moon whose lips, we thought, were sealed.
We bounced off the board in nothing but our linen skin,

sinking, then exploding from the water, buoyant,
young, floating on our backs over depths,

oblivious of how we rhymed with other nakedness.
Afterwards we dripped on towels, listening

to the suburb snore, satisfied that we'd been smart,
had dimmed the patio lights to drape the veil of night

over our frolic. . . until we saw and shrieked: tomorrow's
rumors would be true! We'd left the lights on in the pool!

Saying Good-By to Edith

At the flight gate we were an amoeba trying to absorb Edith,
tugging the sleeves of her traveling suit, vying to hold
her carry-on bag. All the while we railed against her fate—
parents who had numbers tattooed on their skin, so
moving to L.A. from Cleveland no big deal to them—
when suddenly reprieve: the flight delayed, more time
to memorize her black and curly hair, square shoulders,
freckled and impassive face. But by the third delay,
and Edith's farewell flowers wilting, we had to grant
that there were others like us in that place, so when
a voice announced *it's time*, our tears had dried
upon our cheeks, our hands waved slowly
with a bit of boredom through the air, and Edith
shrugged before she climbed into her plane.

THE ANGEL OF DEATH

Tall, thin, and a fabulous dancer,
he wore sharkskin suits, alpaca sweaters,
broke a heart I will not name,
and looked a lot like a young Sinatra.

He died too soon—left wife, four kids—
of cancer. At the funeral, his father spoke.

Is *Holocaust* enough to conjure up the man?
The Rabbi had to sit him down, for he was raining
tears enough to send all Cleveland into arks

with grievances against beleaguered God—
he'd lost most everyone he loved, and now his son.

I wasn't there. I heard. My rose of memory
is how he was in stanza one. My sister's too,
but adds this stroke: a party at his house,
and being assaulted in the bathroom by his friends.

Now slick, resplendent, young, he's walking
toward her in her dreams, a knife-crease
in his pants. He smiles, a perfect gentleman,
and offers her his arm.

Taking an Old Man for a Ride

Newly licensed to drive and bored,
Barb, Fran, and I pull up at a bus stop
to offer people rides. They squint at our faces
giddy with the day's options so richly multiplied
by access to a car, then turn away. It's summer
but it feels like spring, cool and flowering
and green as we are green, and nothing
in our world warns against this lark.

Matching our mood, an old man steps forth,
trying to climb into the front seat on top of us.
We secure him in the back and off we go.
He regales us with news about his family
whom we don't know, then partakes of a little
tell-the-taxi-driver therapy. Lucky for him
he has three, full of sass and opinions
on his bunions and divorcing son.

We drive him home, deposit him. He tells us,
thanks, good-bye, taking with him his body,
diminutive like those of his peers, malnourished
in the old country, then eclipsed by oversized
American offspring, and taking with him his soul,
his accent implying terrors we don't know.

IRENE IN WONDERLAND

The people here have all gone mad,
she thinks, four years old, standing
in line with the last immigrants

to pass through Ellis Island, hearing
English for the first time, her mother
a survivor of the death camps, her father too,

though he is buried in Bavaria: leukemia
after the war, marriage, two little kids.
Her mother needs to find a life,

and will, first cleaning offices in the dead
of night. Holding her mother's skirt, her
little brother's hand, Irene hears babble,

also known as *English*, so steps
into the madness when they land.

FAIR AND BALANCED

I had a friend who's still my friend
although I rarely see her. I mention
her because her breasts were pretty
unsymmetrical. I can't remember
which was bigger, right or left.
But for the sake of balance, let's
say left. Her mother's firstborn
died in Auschwitz. And once I saw
a mournful little photograph
of my friend at four holding her
little brother's hand at the grave
of their father who survived, but
didn't, the war. Yet she isn't sad
or morbid but witty and sweet.
This is what she's like: she used to
take electric rollers with her to the
nursing home where she worked
so she could curl the old ladies' hair.
Being with her is like being at a fair.
Her face is fair. Life isn't fair,
but still my friend can love. What
has all this to do with language, right
and left? Nothing. Unless you let
yourself be tutored by the breast.

OLD/NEW

Early on a Sunday in the world we came of age in,
Barb and I cut through backyards to Sandy's house.

We pass a ginger squirrel flying up a tree. I'm struck
by its hue, for I remember Cleveland squirrels as grey.

Otherwise the neighborhood's the same, its current refugees
not from the particular hell ours knew—they don't have

numbers on their skin—but have fled a place where once
upon a buried resonating time we all set forth on foot to wander.

At Sandy's house her cat strolls by, blasé, a limp chipmunk
sleeping in her dainty mouth. When she lays it down to yawn,

the chipmunk comes alive, zipping under the porch on cue
in nature's strangely written script. The circles widen.

Barb covers her eyes, afraid to see predation's denouement.
I gaze toward a distant maple, powerless to praise

the chipmunk's devotion to its striped little life. But Sandy,
daughter of Holocaust survivors, chases her cat with a broom.

Elsewhere, armies, this we know, are giving certain people
hot feet, forcing them to roam instead of digging gardens deep.

As for us, we hop in Sandy's car and go to JACK'S to eat.

THE WISE GIRLS WALK

All three sisters walked the same—
legs wide apart, hips thrust forward
the way hood ornaments break the highway air;
hips before the chest, its bone cage
surrounding its bird heart;
hips before the face,
its assortment of features;
hips before the mind in its bunker skull;
the hollow between hips forcing the feet
to splay away from the body
like dancer's feet, Janus feet
cleaving the soul, dark from light,
working the legs worked by those avant-garde
hips with which the wise girls walked,
a globe resting between their thighs
and held by their knees aloft—
walked, had to walk, and
had to carry the world there
and not let it fall.

FEEDING THE DOG HALVAH

I need my dog's no-nonsense attitude
mixed with his derangement to help me
edit this book. His icy nose is bracing.
His drowsy eyes with fake fur eyes above
show me how to marry mind asleep to
mind awake, seize opportunities to leap.
I offer a Blue Dog cookie to lure him onto the bed,
my temporary office, his silence a non-distracting
salve for necessary isolation. I've a chunk
of pistachio halvah for me, its sesame texture
like Middle Eastern sand, and a glass of water
to irrigate the poems. He sniffs it out. I share.
It's gone. Then so is he. Exposed for lack
of a wooly undercoat like his, I work the work.

HEART AND SOUL

Here I am in the city of my youth
where I learned to jitterbug so well
my skirts swirled around my legs

one way, then the other, my left hand
on the shoulder of the boy I'm dancing with,
his left holding my right to pull me in

before I fly away altogether. Today,
a zillion years later, I'm with my buddy
Barb in a nursing home visiting her cousin

who happens to be the beautiful woman
whose kids I babysat every Saturday night
before I joined the ranks of dating fools,

she and her handsome husband dressed
to the nines, stepping out. At first, I can't see
her in her bed, just the bars and blankets

she's lost in like Kafka's hunger artist on his
bed of straw. But when she sits up, small
and frail, her face is her face unchanged,

her voice is her voice. I even hear the swish
of bygone taffeta billowing as she rushes
through the living room clasping an earring on.

I'd know her anywhere, and she remembers me,
yon teenager eating every can of potato sticks
in the house. She must also be recalling

those nights of freedom, swaying away
from the grip of domesticity, enjoying the romance
of dressing up and going out, the kids in pajamas

safe with the sitter who lives across the street,
she and her husband returning in the wee hours
to find me weeping at the end of a movie, or asleep.

I'm glad she's Barb's cousin, for that is why
I'm getting to see her at the end of her life,
the three of us joined in a dance, no way

to whirl away. "Heart and Soul" is the one piece
everyone trained or untrained on a piano
can play, my two tugging against each other

like the hands of jitter-buggers spinning out
until they are apart the length of their arms.
But most nights the music is playing,

and under the beat's compulsion, elbows bend,
and the dancers return to each other
no matter their trajectories, irrevocably joined.

Reb Crowsky

Reb Crowsky—Barb says he's Crowsidic—
is davening, a bob for every *caw*, in the bare
branches of his February shul, its doors and
windows open wide and canting heavenward
above alley stones. He can't caw without bobbing,
as if spasming forth prayers from chest, throat,
feathers, devotional mind, his wings
and reptilian feet helping him balance—ha!
crow's feet, etchings of joy!—before pausing,
then *caw*, *caw*, *caw*, daven, daven, daven,
until backyards, a passing train, cat, dog,
we walkers foreshortened are hallowed
by this black cloaked, black hatted chanter
of Midrash pitting his syrinx against gray sky.

Coda

A RIFF ON RABBI HILLEL THE ELDER

That which was hateful to you
do not visit upon Palestinians.
That is the whole Torah;
the rest is commentary.
Now go and learn.

~

"if it is not / safe for some / it is not / for anyone"
    Matthew Zapruder, "December" (from *Father's Day*)

NOTES

"April Fools" page 5: "Little girls climbing into school buses" is for all the brave Malalas risking their lives for an education. "Doctors and nurses heading straight for rubble and plagues" is for all the courageous Doctors Without Borders treating patients, and the White Helmets digging through the rubble of bombed buildings for survivors. "Anonymous artists writing on barrier walls" is for the extraordinary graffiti artists drawing on all walls that divide people, including the West Bank barrier wall.

"Unobservant Jew" page 6 borrows from Transcendentalism's theory of the *oversoul* positing the unity of all people and nature. It also borrows from a tale in *Zen Flesh, Zen Bones*, writings compiled by Paul Reps, about an umbrella and a master's question.

"The Burial of Bruno Schulz" page 8: Bruno Schulz, the "Polish Kafka," Jewish artist, teacher, and writer, was murdered on a street in Drohobycz during the Nazi occupation. Some of his manuscripts and murals have never been found. Cart horses were a frequent motif in his work.

"Kafka's Sister" page 9: Kafka died before the rise of Hitler and the invasion of Czechoslovakia, though some read *The Metamorphosis* as a premonition. His sister Ottla died in Auschwitz.

"Saga of Mice" page 11: Art Spiegelman's *Maus*, published in 1986, uses animal fable tradition in order to tell the untellable story of the Holocaust. It ends at the gates of Auschwitz. *Maus II*, 1991, continues his parents' story through Auschwitz/Birkenau and beyond. It won the Pulitzer Prize in 1992.

"After 'After Apple-Picking'" page 14 refers to Robert Frost's poem. *T.A.* is short for *teaching assistant*, a graduate student who teaches courses or grades papers in exchange for a fee waiver.

"Gardenias" page 16: "those guys" are, of course, the Marx brothers.

"Sonnet for Bears": page 19: *Shoah*, Hebrew for *calamity*, is another name for *Holocaust*, Greek for burnt offering.

"Sasha and the Bees" page 20: Gimpel, protagonist of Isaac Singer's "Gimpel the Fool," says, "I wanted to be angry, but that's my misfortune exactly, I don't have it in me to be really angry." He is a Holy Fool.

"Nexus," page 21 was written during the devastating IDF bombing of Gaza in 2014. According to United Nations figures, 2,251 Palestinians died, including 1,462 civilians. 551 were children, 299 women. Six Israeli civilians and 67 Israeli soldiers perished as well. T.S. Eliot coined the phrase, *objective correlative*, to name "a set of objects, a situation, a chain of events which shall be the formular of that particular emotion." That's what the wasp is.

"Rhonda is Staring at Me" page 24: *The Blue Mountain* in the epigraph is a novel about an idealistic Jewish collective farm in Palestine at the turn of the previous century.

"Trapped in the Mirror" page 32: See Lewis Carroll's *Through the Looking Glass* and Jean Cocteau's *Orpheus* for depictions of mirrors as portals to other worlds.

"When Dreams Begin Responsibility," page 34 bears a title inspired by Michael Harper's poem, "Nightmare Begins Responsibility," whose title was in turn inspired by William Butler Yeats' "In Dreams Begin Responsibilities." Delmore Schwartz, also under the sway of Yeats, titled a short story "In Dreams Begin Responsibilities."

"Call Me Ishmael" page 40: Herman Melville's *Moby Dick* begins with this epigraph: *"The Biblical Ishmael, son of Abraham by the slave Hagar, was sent forth into the wilderness with his mother because of the jealousy of Sarah, Abraham's wife, on behalf of her own son Isaac."* The prologue to the Jewish/Palestinian tragedy unfolds in *Genesis 16, 17, 21,* & *25*, with the birth of Ishmael, Abraham's first son. Genesis 16:12, *KJV* says of Ishmael, "his hand *will be* against every man."

"They Tell Me My Grandfather" page 43: The Katzenjammer Kids were mischievous brothers in a comic strip created by Rudolph Dirks in 1897.

"Song of the Shield" page 52 was inspired by local news of a twenty-three-year-old woman, Sanikqua Hester, living on Lilley Avenue in Columbus, Ohio, who gave her life shielding a fourteen-year-old boy from a barrage of bullets from a high-powered rifle.

"When I Opened the Door" page 53 resulted from playing the Surrealist game, "Would You Open the Door?" with my students. Here is the game paraphrased: You are dreaming, hear a knock on the door, open it. Recognizing the visitor, you must decide: either let the visitor enter or close the door. What do you decide? Why?

"Christine on The Days of Awe" page 56: On the High Holy Days of Rosh Hashanah and Yom Kippur, Jewish children don't go to school.

"The Demiurge's Botch" page 57: In Gnostic philosophy Demiurges, ranked below God, created the physical universe. Clearly they made great wonder and beauty, but with what seems to me a deep flaw and why I invoked Allen Ginsburg's *Howl* at the poem's end.

"Do the Right Thing" page 58: The phrase *Hamilton electors* reminds us that if a despot or huckster wins the presidential election, a state's electors may cast votes for a candidate other than the one they are pledged to. The poem also alludes to film director Spike Lee and poet W. H. Auden, whose phrases transcend the need for glossing.

"Saint Kitchen" page 61: In the final third, the poem mentions America's Beats, specifically as represented in Jack Kerouac's *On the Road*.

"Blessing the Sun" page 62: On April 8, 2009, an otherworldly light streamed in through our east-facing front window, sanctifying everything it touched and inspiring the poem. I learned weeks later it happened on the exact date of the Hebrew Blessing of the Sun, recited once every twenty-eight years at the completion of the sun's cycle.

"They are Running to My Mother" page 67 mentions *Uncle Tom's Cabin's* Eliza on her way to Canada across a frozen lake, pursued by slave catchers yet escaping slavery with her son Harry to prevent him from being sold away from her.

"Visitation" page 68: In Jean Cocteau's film *Orphee* (*Orpheus*) the poet has a theological discussion with members of the underworld tribunal. He is trying to retrieve his wife Euridice, but also to see the gaunt and beautiful Princess, his personal Death, with whom he is in love.

"Odessa Pogrom" page 73: A Christian neighbor hid my maternal grandmother, Leah Himmelfarb Kobrinsky, in her attic during a pogrom in Ukraine. I imagine Leah pregnant, the event from her point of view. The image of drunken men beating horses in the snow migrated to my imagination from a scene in Dostoevsky's *Crime and Punishment*. It seems to be a motif in Russian literature.

"Piggy" page 77: Thanks to daughter Sonya for comparing my sister Laura and me to the two-headed monster on *Sesame Street* (and to *Sesame Street* for holding up that mirror.)

"Idly By" page 81 mentions "Hal," the computer with a will in Kubrick's *2001: A Space Odyssey*. Was the audible breathing in the film Hal's, or was it Dr. David Bowman's (Keir Dullea's). Perhaps the breather's identity is deliberately and metaphorically ambiguous in the film.

"Swimming with Margie On and Off the Road to Heaven" page 101: The SS cynically and perversely referred to the path to the gas chambers at Sobibor, Treblinka, and Auschwitz as *the road to heaven*. Some inmates took it up as well. In "Lady Lazarus, Sylvia Plath refers to her face as "a featureless fine / Jew linen."

"Heart and Soul" page 110 contains a brief allusion to the protagonist in Franz Kafka's short story, "The Hunger Artist."

Glossary of Yiddish terms used in the poems:

charoset: sticky sweet symbolic Passover food, usually apples, honey, nuts, wine.
daven: pray, sometimes while rocking.
fress: eat.
golem: clay figure brought to life by magic.
Haggadah: text recited at Passover seder.
hosanna: expression of praise.
Kaddish: mourning prayer.
kneydlekh: matzah ball.
kvell: burst with joy, pride.
maven: expert.
mechaieh: a pleasure, joy.
Midrash: commentary on Biblical text.
mishegoss: craziness
mishpocha: relatives by blood or marriage.
Mizrahi: Jews from Middle East or North Africa.
Moishele: affectionate diminutive for Moses.
Rosh Hashanah: Jewish new year.
schlep: haul or carry.
schmatta: rag, cloth.
schmooze: easy-going chat, talk.
shofar: a ram's horn blown like a trumpet on Rosh Hashana and Yom Kippur.
shul: synagogue.
tallit: fringed religious shawl.
Tashlich: symbolic casting off of sins on Rosh Hashanah by throwing bread into a
      river or lake.
tchotchke: small decorative object.
tsibele: onion.
tuchus: butt, bum, rear end.
yarmulke: skullcap.
yiddishe: Jewish.
Yom Kippur: Jewish day of atonement, a fast day, sundown to sundown.

ACKNOWLEDGMENTS

Thanks to the editors of the following magazines and anthologies for publishing these poems, some in earlier iterations:

"Africa Party," *Rattle*
"April Fools," *Forklift Ohio*
"Blessing the Sun," *Tomorrow and Tomorrow*
"Bread," *Poetica magazine*
"The Burial of Bruno Schulz," *Hotel Amerika*
"Burning Bush," *Birmingham Poetry Review*
"Call Me Ishmael," *Pudding magazine*
"Country and Country," *Mudfish*
"Do the Right Thing," *The Columbus Anthology* (Ohio State University Press, Amanda Page, Editor)
"Ducks," *Common Threads*
"Fair and Balanced," *Madness Muse Press* #3
"Fiasco Under an Impeccable March Sky," *The Ides of March: An Anthology of Ohio Poets* (Columbus Creative Cooperative, Hannah Stephenson, Editor)
"Gardenias," *Rattle*
"Heart and Soul," *What but the Music* (anthology, Gelles-Cole Literary Enterprises, Kenneth Saltzmann, Editor)
"Idly By," *Mudfish*
"Irene in Wonderland," *Pudding magazine*
"Kafka's Sister," *Heartlands*
"Last Repast," *Hot One*, a chapbook from House of Toast Poets
"Let's Eat the Delicious Potatoes," *Pudding magazine*
"Look at the Sea," *Poem for Cleveland* (anthology, Ray McNiece, Editor)
"Maria," *Botticelli magazine*
"Miracle of the Mass," *Metamorphosis*, Ohio Writers Association anthology
"Middle East Shadow," *Poetry in the Park* chapbook
"Mother Leaves the Bardo," *Vincent Brothers Review*
"My Father, Art, In Heaven," *Coffeehouse Poets*, a chapbook
"Old/New," *Poem for Cleveland* (anthology, Ray McNiece, Editor)
"Onions," *Literary Imagination*
"Piggy," *Botticelli magazine*
"Rag Man's Sons," *Vincent Brothers Review*
"Reb Crowsky," *Poetica magazine*
"Saint Kitchen," *Tomorrow and Tomorrow*
"The Song of the Shield," *Pudding magazine: Killer Poems*
"Sunday School," *Pudding magazine*
"They are Running to My Mother," *Not My President*, an anthology from Thoughtcrimes Press. Reprinted in *Common Threads*, 2019
"They Tell Me My Grandfather," *Poetica magazine*
"They Thought Our Sins Were Bread," *The Manhattan Review*. Nominated for a Pushcart Prize.

"Unobservant Jew," *The Pudding House Gang* (anthology, Pudding House Publications)

"Visitation," *The Poet's Quest for God: Contemporary Poems of Faith, Doubt, and Wonder*, Eyewear Publications

"You Carried Her in Your Arms," *Jewish Literary Journal*

∽

"Saint Kitchen," honorable mention from Ilya Kaminsky, Poetry Society of America Lyric Poetry Award, 2019.

"Burning Bush" appeared in *Flowering Bruno: A Dography* (XOXOX Press). "Country and Country" and "The Demiurge's Botch" appeared in *Taking a Walk in My Animal Hat* (Bottom Dog Press)

"Saga of Mice" appeared in *Mischief,* a chapbook of poems (Pudding House). "Saga of Mice," "Deputized," "*Ivanhoe*," and "The Burial of Bruno Schulz," appeared in *Frankenstein's Flowers* (CW Books 2014) [out of print, available from the author].

"The Wise Girls Walk" is etched in braille on Todd Slaughter's *Vanitas*, a sculpture in the atrium of the Columbus Metropolitan Library, Columbus, Ohio.

∽

Thanks for suggestions on many of these poems from poets MJ Abell, Fred Andrle, Linda Fuller-Smith, Jerry Roscoe, Jacquelin Smith, Geoff Anderson, Rose Smith, and Karen Scott, and thanks to my "rabbi" Farrell Brody for wisdom and clarity. I am grateful to Eleanor Wilner, Philip Terman, and Philip Metres for their insights and generous blurbs, and to poets Mary Crow, Rae Armantrout, Stanley Moss, Matthew Zapruder, and the estate of Howard Nemerov for permission to quote from works. Various filmmakers, singers, authors, poets, theologians, and mystics have influenced these poems, so I thank them too, as I do my husband Patrick, my adult children Madeleine, Sonya, and Daniel, Dan's wife Sharon, my departed stepson Eric, and my grandchildren Kip and Joshua, for companionship and inspiration. Thanks to serial dogs and cats Ribby, Bruno, Kizzy, Sasha, Rhonda, and Harpo for similar. I'm grateful to my departed parents Arthur Cohen and Anne Kobrinsky Cohen for the gift of my being, my heritage, and my glorious *mishpocha*. Many thanks to the neighborhood where I grew up, South Euclid, Ohio, a suburb of Cleveland, teeming with children born after WWII, for memories and life-long friendships. And thank you Waterville, Maine and Winnipeg, Manitoba, for nurturing my parents to adulthood.

Huge thanks to my cousin Nora Kobrinsky, Winnipeg artist, for letting us reproduce her dreamy, joyful, bright, resonant, and beautiful painting, *Golden Afternoon*, on the cover of *Jewgirl*.

ABOUT THE AUTHOR

Charlene had a pretty secular upbringing notwithstanding her maiden name of Cohen, so how did this book happen? She sang about the complex emotional and political legacy of the particularity into which she was born, returned often to that venerable, contradictory, joyful, angsty *mishegoss*, gathered the poems. An Emeritus Professor of English at Columbus College of Art and Design, Charlene co-coordinates Hospital Poets at the Ohio State University hospitals, and, motivated by the suffering of her own people, works for peace and justice for those whose suffering is akin. Charlene has received awards from The Poetry Society of America as well as the Ohio and Greater Columbus Arts Councils, and was a featured author at The Thurber House and The Ohioana Book Festival. She is mother of three and grandmother of two, has too many books yet keeps checking out more from the library, isn't a very good gardener but likes to toss seeds around to see what transpires, and hikes too. While growing up she heard *Jewgirl* used as an insider term, but if it has a sting, she appropriates the whole shebang. Her website is https://charlenefix.com